ISBN 978-0-267-00083-8
PIBN 10797367

THE SILVER SONG SERIES No. 13.

SACRED SONGS

FOR

SCHOOL USE.

Compiled and Arranged by

MILTON Z. TINKER,

Director of Music in the Public Schools, Evansville, Indiana.

SILVER, BURDETT & COMPANY,

New York.   Boston.   Chicago.

THE SILVER SONG SERIES.

Other Volumes in Preparation.

SILVER, BURDETT & COMPANY,

NEW YORK.   BOSTON.   CHICAGO.

PUBLISHERS' NOTE.

THE SILVER SONG SERIES affords a succession of carefully edited, well graded books, containing songs particularly adapted for recreative use, and supplemental to the song material found in the regular music readers. Each book is complete in itself, and each contains a wide variety of songs of the highest order, embracing patriotic, devotional, occasional and miscellaneous songs,—all carefully arranged to fall clearly within the limits of the pupil's musical possibilities, at the several stages.

The hymn and tunes in the present collection have been brought together with a view to furnishing, in convenient and inexpensive form, a book for use in devotional exercises in high schools and academies. They include many of the favorite and classic hymns which should become familiar in school days. Due regard is had to the conditions in public schools and the need of selections which shall be universally acceptable.

It is hoped that the number and variety of the hymns, their quality and their appropriateness, will commend the book.

SACRED SONGS.

The Silver Song Series No. 13.

ERNAN. 10s.   LOWELL MASON.

Oh, come, and let us all, with one ac - cord, Lift up our cheer - ful voice, and praise the Lord!

Let us this eve - ning bless His ho - ly Name, Yes, let us laud and mag - ni - fy the same.

1   Evening Worship.

OH, come, and let us all, with one accord,
Lift up our cheerful voice, and praise the
    Lord!
Let us this evening bless His holy Name,
Yea, let us laud and magnify the same.

2 Let universal nature ever raise
A cheerful voice to give Him thanks and
    praise;
Let us and all His saints His glory sing,
Who is our blessèd Saviour, Lord, and
    King.

3 Therefore let all in heaven and earth
    agree
To sing His praise in perfect unity;
Yea, let His servants all, with one accord,
With joyful hallelujahs praise the Lord.
                ANON. Ps. 95

2   Psalm 42.

AS PANTS the wearied hart for cooling
    springs,   [chase,
That sinks exhausted in the summer's
So pants my soul for Thee, great King of
    kings,   [place.
So thirsts to reach Thy sacred dwelling-

2 Why throb, my heart? why sink, my
    saddening soul?   [oppressed?
Why droop to earth with various woes
My years shall yet in blissful circles roll,
  My peace be yet an inmate of this breast.

3 Lord, Thy sure mercies, ever in my sight,
My heart shall gladden through the te-
    dious day;
And, midst the dark and gloomy shades of
    night,   [lay.
To Thee, my God, I'll tune the grateful
                ROBERT LOWTH.

MORNINGTON.   S. M.   Arr. by L. Mason.

Lord, bid Thy light a - rise   On   all Thy   peo - ple   here,

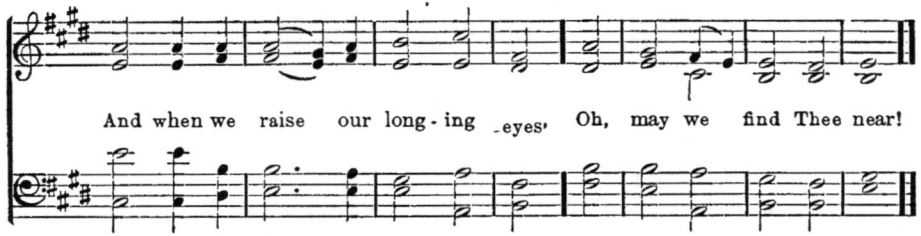

And when we   raise   our long - ing _eyes,   Oh, may we   find Thee near!

3   The Light.

Lord, bid Thy light arise
  On all Thy people here,
And when we raise our longing eyes,
  Oh, may we find Thee near!

2 Thy Holy Spirit send,
  To quicken every soul;
And hearts, the most rebellious, bend
  To Thy divine control.

3 Let all that own Thy name
  Thy sacred image bear,
And light in every heart the flame
  Of watchfulness and prayer.

4 Since in Thy love we see
  Our only sure relief,
Oh, raise our earthly minds to Thee,
  And help our unbelief!
                      W. H. Bathurst.

4   Teaching Truth.

Come, Spirit, source of light,
  Thy grace is unconfined;
Dispel the gloomy shades of night,
  The darkness of the mind.

2 Now to our eyes display
  The truth Thy words reveal;
Cause us to run the heavenly way,
  Delighting in Thy will.

3 Thy teachings make us know
  The mysteries of Thy love,
The vanity of things below,
  The joy of things above.

4 While through this maze we stray,
  Oh, spread Thy beams abroad;
Disclose the dangers of the way,
  And guide our steps to God.
                      B. Beddome, alt.

HENDON. 7s.   C. MALAN.

LORD, we come be - fore Thee now, At Thy feet we hum-bly bow;

Oh, do not our suit dis - dain! Shall we seek Thee, Lord, in vain?

Shall we seek Thee, Lord, in vain?

5   "Thy face we seek."

LORD, we come before Thee now,
At Thy feet we humbly bow;
Oh, do not our suit disdain!
Shall we seek Thee, Lord, in vain?

2 Lord, on Thee our souls depend,
In compassion now descend;
Fill our hearts with Thy rich grace,
Tune our lips to sing Thy praise.

3 Comfort those who weep and mourn:
Let the time of joy return;
Those that are cast down lift up;
Make them strong in faith and hope.

4 Grant that all may seek and find
Thee a God supremely kind;
Heal the sick; the captive free;
Let us all rejoice in Thee.
                                    WILLIAM HAMMOND.

6   "The Everlasting Arms."

EVERLASTING arms of love
Are beneath, around, above;
He who left His throne of light,
And unnumbered angels bright;—

2 He who on the accursèd tree
Gave His precious life for me;
He it is that bears me on,
His the arm I lean upon.

3 All things hasten to decay,
Earth and sea will pass away;
Soon will yonder circling sun
Cease his blazing course to run.

4 Scenes will vary, friends grow strange,
But the Changeless cannot change:
Gladly will I journey on,
With His arm to lean upon.
                                    JOHN R. MACDUFF.

HURSLEY. L. M.   Arr. by W. H. MONK.

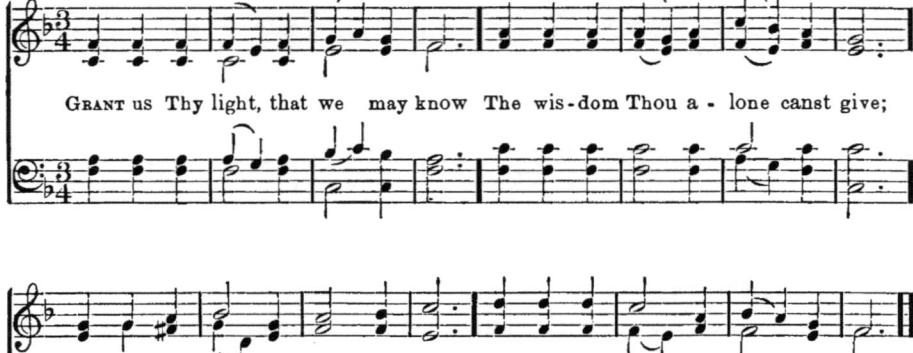

Grant us Thy light, that we may know The wis-dom Thou a - lone canst give;

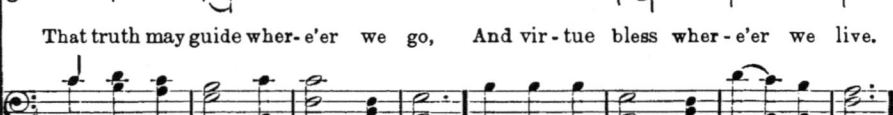

That truth may guide wher-e'er we go, And vir-tue bless wher-e'er we live.

7   In the Light of God.

GRANT us Thy light, that we may know
  The wisdom Thou alone canst give;
That truth may guide where'er we go,
  And virtue bless where'er we live.

2 Grant us Thy light, that we may see
  Where error lurks in human lore,
And turn our doubting minds to Thee,
  And love Thy simple word the more.

3 Grant us Thy light, that we may learn
  How dead is life from Thee apart;
How sure is joy for all who turn
  To Thee an undivided heart.

4 Grant us Thy light, in grief and pain,
  To lift our burdened hearts above;
And count the very cross a gain,
  And bless our Father's hidden love.
                                    ANON.

8   Contentment.

O LORD, how full of sweet content
Our years of pilgrimage are spent!
Where'er we dwell, we dwell with Thee,
In heaven, in earth, or on the sea.

2 To us remains nor place nor time:
Our country is in every clime:
We can be calm and free from care
On any shore, since God is there.

3 While place we seek, or place we shun,
The soul finds happiness in none;
But with our God to guide our way,
'T is equal joy to go or stay.

4 Could we be cast where Thou art not,
That were indeed a dreadful lot;
But regions none remote we call,
Secure of finding God in all.
                          WILLIAM COWPER, tr.

WARE. L. M.   GEO. KINGSLEY.

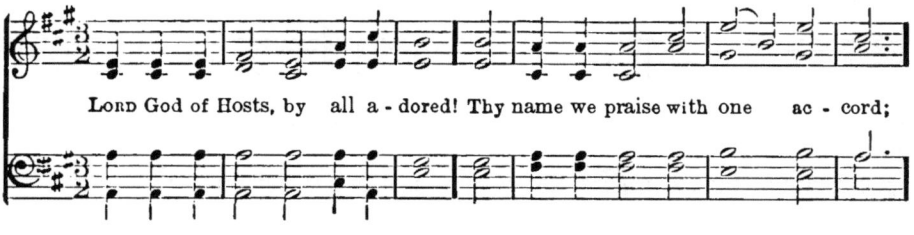

Lord God of Hosts, by all a - dored! Thy name we praise with one ac - cord;

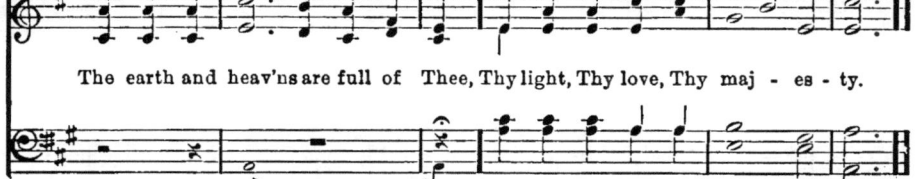

The earth and heav'ns are full of Thee, Thy light, Thy love, Thy maj - es - ty.

9   "Te Deum."

Lord God of Hosts, by all adored!
Thy name we praise with one accord;
The earth and heavens are full of Thee,
Thy light, Thy love, Thy majesty.

2 Loud hallelujahs to Thy name
Angels and seraphim proclaim;
Eternal praise to Thee is given
By all the powers and thrones in heaven.

3 The holy church in every place
Throughout the world exalts Thy praise;
Both heaven and earth do worship Thee,
Thou Father of eternity!

4 From day to day, O Lord, do we
Highly exalt and honor Thee;

Thy name we worship and adore,
World without end for evermore.
                      JOHN GAMBOLD, alt.

10   "Perpetual blessings."

My God, how endless is Thy love
Thy gifts are every evening new;
And morning mercies, from above,
Gently distill, like early dew.

2 Thou spread'st the curtains of the night,
Great Guardian of my sleeping hours;
Thy sovereign word restores the light,
And quickens all my drowsy powers.

3 I yield my powers to Thy command;
To Thee I consecrate my days;
Perpetual blessings from Thy hand
Demand perpetual songs of praise.
                      ISAAC WATTS.

SILVER STREET. S. M.   I. SMITH.

Come, sound His praise a - broad, And hymns of glo - ry sing:

Je - ho - vah is the sov - 'reign God, The u - ni - ver - sal King.

11   Psalm 95.

COME, sound His praise abroad,
  And hymns of glory sing:
Jehovah is the sovereign God,
  The universal King.

2 He formed the deeps unknown;
  He gave the seas their bound;
The watery worlds are all His own,
  And all the solid ground.

3 Come, worship at His throne,
  Come, bow before the Lord:
We are His work, and not our own,
  He formed us by His word.

4 To-day attend His voice,
  Nor dare provoke His rod;
Come, like the people of His choice,
  And own our gracious God.
                                ISAAC WATTS.

12   "Bless the Lord."

STAND up, and bless the Lord,
  Ye people of His choice;
Stand up, and bless the Lord your God,
  With heart and soul and voice.

2 Though high above all praise,
  Above all blessing high,
Who would not fear His holy name,
  And laud, and magnify?

3 Oh, for the living flame
  From His own altar brought,
To touch our lips, our souls inspire,
  And wing to heaven our thought!

4 Stand up, and bless the Lord;
  The Lord your God adore;
Stand up, and bless His glorious name,
  Henceforth, for evermore.
                         JAMES MONTGOMERY.

ELIZABETHTOWN. C. M.   GEO. KINGSLEY.

Thou grace di-vine en - cir-cling all,   A   sound-less, shoreless   sea!

Where-in   at   last   our   souls must   fall,   O   Love of   God most free!

13   Grace Divine.

Thou grace divine encircling all,
  A soundless, shoreless sea!
Wherein at last our souls must fall,
  O Love of God most free!

2 And though we turn us from Thy face,
  And wander wide and long,
Thou hold'st us still in Thine embrace,
  O Love of God most strong!

3 The saddened heart, the restless soul,
  The toil-worn frame and mind,
Alike confess Thy sweet control,
  O Love of God most kind!

4 And filled and quickened by Thy breath,
  Our souls are strong and free
To rise o'er sin and fear and death,
  O Love of God, to Thee!

                    ELIZA SCUDDER

14   In Nature.

Lord, when my raptured thought surveys
  Creation's beauties o'er,
All nature joins to teach Thy praise,
  And bid my soul adore.

2 Where'er I turn my gazing eyes,
  Thy radiant footsteps shine;
Ten thousand pleasing wonders rise,
  And speak their source divine.

3 On me Thy providence has shone
  With gentle smiling rays;
Oh, let my lips and life make known
  Thy goodness and Thy praise.

4 All-bounteous Lord, Thy grace impart!
  Oh, teach me to improve
Thy gifts with humble, grateful heart,
  And crown them with Thy love.

                    ANNE STEELE.

VESPER HYMN. 8s, 7s. D.   Arr. by L. Mason.

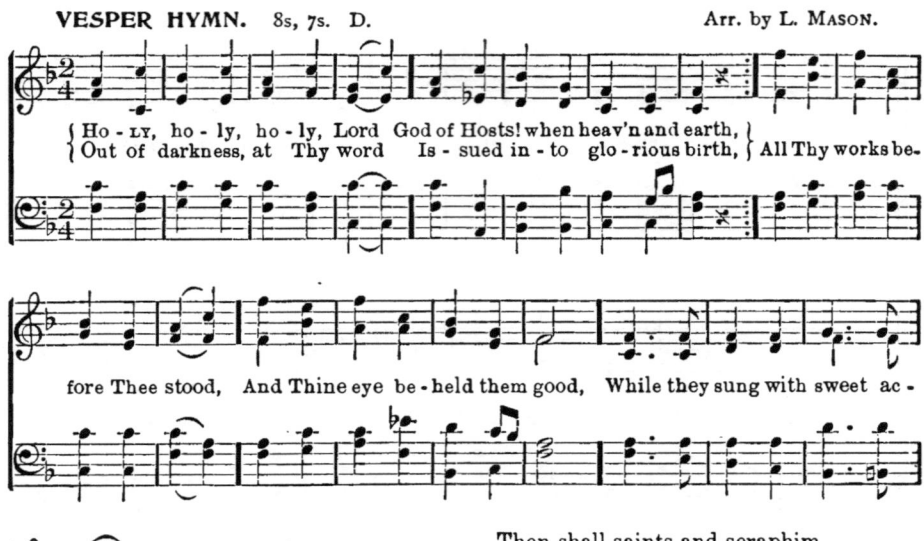

{ Ho - ly, ho - ly, ho - ly, Lord God of Hosts! when heav'n and earth, }
{ Out of darkness, at Thy word Is - sued in - to glo - rious birth, } All Thy works be-

fore Thee stood, And Thine eye be - held them good, While they sung with sweet ac -

cord, Ho - ly, ho - ly, ho - ly Lord!

15   "Holy, holy, holy."

HOLY, holy, holy, Lord
  God of Hosts! when heaven and earth,
Out of darkness, at Thy word
  Issued into glorious birth,
All Thy works before Thee stood,
And Thine eye beheld them good,
While they sung with sweet accord,
Holy, holy, holy Lord!

2 Holy, holy, holy! all
  Heaven's triumphant choir shall sing,
While the ransomed nations fall
  At the footstool of their King:

Then shall saints and seraphim,
Harps and voices, swell one hymn,
Blending in sublime accord,
Holy, holy, holy Lord!
                        JAMES MONTGOMERY.

16   Divine Presence.

LORD of earth! Thy forming hand
Well this beauteous frame hath planned;
Woods that wave, and hills that tower,
Ocean rolling in his power:
Yet, amid this scene so fair,
Should I cease Thy smile to share,
What were all its joys to me?
Whom have I on earth but Thee?

2 Lord of heaven! beyond our sight
Shines a world of purer light;
There in love's unclouded reign
Parted hands shall meet again:
Oh, that world is passing fair!
Yet, if Thou wert absent there,
What were all its joys to me?
Whom have I in heaven but Thee?
                        ROBERT GRANT.

MIRIAM. 7s, 6s. D.   J. P. HOLBROOK.

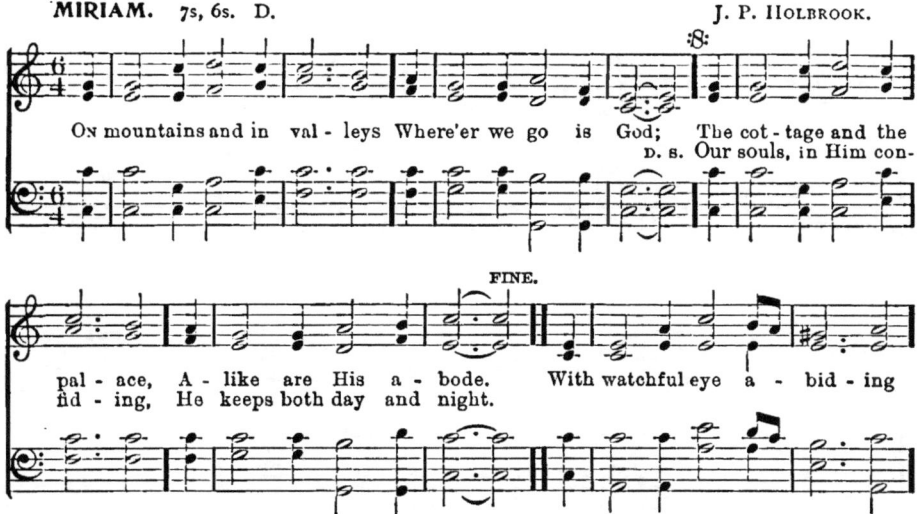

On mountains and in val - leys Where'er we go is God; The cot - tage and the

D. s. Our souls, in Him con-

pal - ace, A - like are His a - bode. With watchful eye a - bid - ing
fid - ing, He keeps both day and night.

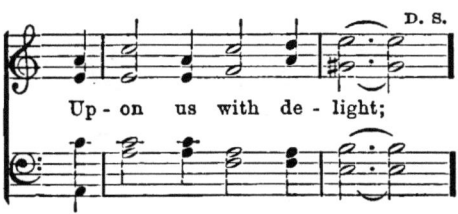

Up - on us with de - light;

17   Omnipresent.

On mountains and in valleys
  Where'er we go is God;
The cottage and the palace,
  Alike are His abode.
With watchful eye abiding
  Upon us with delight;
Our souls, in Him confiding,
  He keeps both day and night.

2 Above me and beside me,
  My God is ever near,
To watch, protect, and guide me,
  Whatever ills appear.

Though other friends may fail me;
  In sorrow's dark abode,
Though death itself assail me,
  I'm ever safe with God.
           Tr. fr. the Dutch.

18   Sovereign Love.

'Tis not that I did choose Thee,
  For, Lord! that could not be;
This heart would still refuse Thee;
  But Thou hast chosen me;—
Hast, from the sin that stained me,
  Washed me and set me free,
And to this end ordained me,
  That I should live to Thee.

2 'Twas sovereign mercy called me,
  And taught my opening mind;
The world had else enthralled me,
  To heavenly glories blind.
My heart owns none above Thee;
  For Thy rich grace I thirst;
This knowing,—if I love Thee,
  Thou must have loved me first.
           Josiah Conder

DWIGHT. L. M.   Arr. fr. BELLINI.

O LOVE Di-vine! that stooped to share   Our sharpest pang, our bit-t'rest tear,

On Thee we cast each earth-born care,   We smile at pain, while Thou art near.

19   "Thou art near."   .

O LOVE Divine! that stooped to share
  Our sharpest pang, our bitterest tear,
On Thee we cast each earth-born care,
  We smile at pain, while Thou art near.

2 Though long the weary way we tread,
  And sorrow crown each lingering year,
No path we shun, no darkness dread,
  Our hearts still whispering, Thou art
    near.

3 When drooping pleasure turns to grief,
  And trembling faith is changed to fear,
The murmuring wind, the quivering leaf,
  Shall softly tell us Thou art near.

4 On Thee we fling our burdening woe,
  O Love Divine, forever dear;

Content to suffer while we know,
  Living or dying, Thou art near!
                        O. W. HOLMES.

20   Divine Providence.

GOD of the world! Thy glories shine,
Through earth and heaven with rays divine;
Thy smile gives beauty to the flower,
Thine anger to the tempest power.

2 God of eternal life! Thy love
Doth every stain of sin remove;
The cross, the cross,—its hallowed light
Shall drive from earth her cheerless night.

3 God of all goodness! to the skies
Our hearts in grateful anthems rise;
And to Thy service shall be given
The rest of life, the whole of heaven.
                        S. S. CUTTING.

LOUVAN.   L. M.   V. C. TAYLOR.

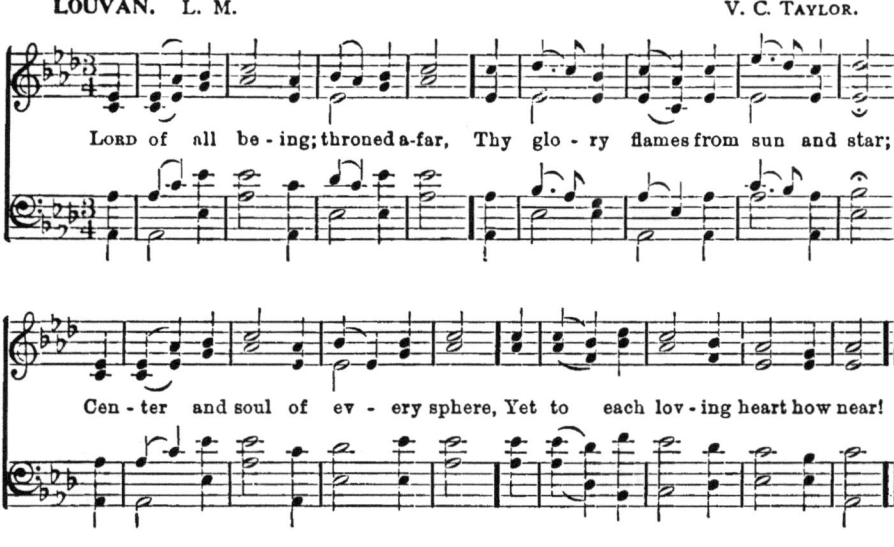

Lord of all be-ing; throned a-far, Thy glo-ry flames from sun and star;

Cen-ter and soul of ev-ery sphere, Yet to each lov-ing heart how near!

21   Omnipresence.

Lord of all being; throned afar,
Thy glory flames from sun and star;
Center and soul of every sphere,
Yet to each loving heart how near!

2 Sun of our life, Thy quickening ray
Sheds on our path the glow of day;
Star of our hope, Thy softened light
Cheers the long watches of the night.

3 Our midnight is Thy smile withdrawn;
Our noontide is Thy gracious dawn;
Our rainbow arch Thy mercy's sign;
All, save the clouds of sin, are Thine!

4 Lord of all life, below, above,
Whose light is truth, whose warmth is love,
Before Thy ever-blazing throne
We ask no luster of our own.

ANON.

22   Sovereignty.

Lord, my weak thought in vain would climb
To search the starry vault profound;
In vain would wing her flight sublime,
To find creation's outmost bound.

2 But weaker yet that thought must prove
To search Thy great eternal plan,—
Thy sovereign counsels, born of love
Long ages ere the world began.

3 When my dim reason would demand
Why that, or this, Thou dost ordain,
By some vast deep I seem to stand,
Whose secrets I must ask in vain.

4 When doubts disturb my troubled breast,
And all is dark as night to me,
Here, as on solid rock, I rest;
That so it seemeth good to Thee.

ANON.

VARINA.   C. M. D.   G. F. Root, arr.

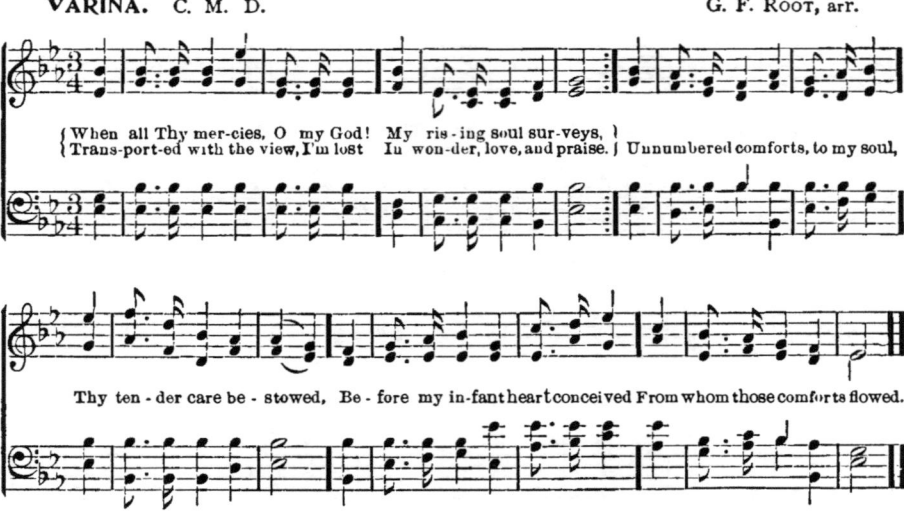

{ When all Thy mer-cies, O my God! My ris-ing soul sur-veys, }
{ Trans-port-ed with the view, I'm lost In won-der, love, and praise. } Unnumbered comforts, to my soul,

Thy ten-der care be-stowed, Be-fore my in-fant heart conceived From whom those comforts flowed.

23   Continued Help.

WHEN all Thy mercies, O my God!
  My rising soul surveys,
Transported with the view, I'm lost
  In wonder, love, and praise.
Unnumbered comforts, to my soul,
  Thy tender care bestowed,
Before my infant heart conceived
  From whom those comforts flowed.

2 When, in the slippery paths of youth,
  With heedless steps, I ran,
Thine arm, unseen, conveyed me safe,
  And led me up to man.
Ten thousand, thousand precious gifts
  My daily thanks employ;
Nor is the least a cheerful heart,
  That tastes those gifts with joy.

3 Through every period of my life,
  Thy goodness I'll pursue;
And after death, in distant worlds,
  The glorious theme renew.

Through all eternity, to Thee
  A joyful song I'll raise;
For, oh, eternity's too short
  To utter all Thy praise!
                        JOSEPH ADDISON.

24   Psalm 90.

OUR God, our help in ages past,
  Our hope for years to come;
Our shelter from the stormy blast,
  And our eternal home!
Under the shadow of Thy throne
  Thy saints have dwelt secure;
Sufficient is Thine arm alone,
  And our defence is sure.

2 Before the hills in order stood,
  Or earth received her frame,
From everlasting Thou art God,
  To endless years the same.
A thousand ages, in Thy sight,
  Are like an evening gone;
Short as the watch that ends the night,
  Before the rising sun.

3 Time, like an ever-rolling stream
  Bears all its sons away;
They fly, forgotten, as a dream
  Dies at the opening day.

Our God, our help in ages past,
  Our hope for years to come,
Be Thou our guard while troubles last,
  And our eternal home.

ISAAC WATTS.

DUNDEE. C. M.

G. FRANC.

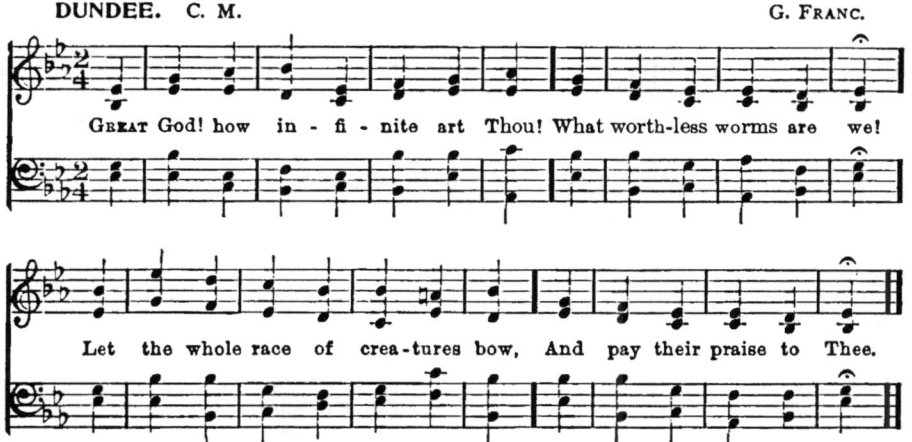

25   Eternity.

GREAT God! how infinite art Thou!
  What worthless worms are we!
Let the whole race of creatures bow,
  And pay their praise to Thee.

2 Thy throne eternal ages stood,
  Ere seas or stars were made:
Thou art the ever-living God,
  Were all the nations dead.

3 Eternity, with all its years,
  Stands present in Thy view;
To Thee there's nothing old appears—
  Great God! there's nothing new.

4 Our lives through various scenes are drawn,
  And vexed with trifling cares;
While Thine eternal thought moves on
  Thine undisturbed affairs.

ANON.

26   Omnipresence.

IN all my vast concerns with Thee,
  In vain my soul would try
To shun Thy presence, Lord! or flee
  The notice of Thine eye.

2 Thine all-surrounding sight surveys
  My rising and my rest,
My public walks, my private ways,
  And secrets of my breast.

3 My thoughts lie open to the Lord,
  Before they're formed within;
And, ere my lips pronounce the word,
  He knows the sense I mean.

4 Oh, wondrous knowledge, deep and high,
  Where can a creature hide?
Within Thy circling arms I lie,
  Enclosed on every side.

ANON.

ITALIAN HYMN.   6s, 4s.   F. GIARDINI.

COME, Thou Al-might-y King, Help us Thy name to sing, Help us to praise: { Father ! all-glo-ri-ous, } { O'er all vic-to-ri-ous, }

Come, and reign o-ver us, Ancient of Days!

27   "One in Three."

COME, Thou Almighty King,
Help us Thy name to sing,
  Help us to praise:
Father! all-glorious,
O'er all victorious,
Come, and reign over us,
  Ancient of Days!

2 Come, Thou incarnate Word,
Gird on Thy mighty sword;
  Our prayer attend;
Come, and Thy people bless,
And give Thy word success,
Spirit of holiness!
  On us descend.

3 Come, holy Comforter!
Thy sacred witness bear,
  In this glad hour:

Thou, who almighty art,
Now rule in every heart,
And ne'er from us depart,
  Spirit of power!

               ANON.

28   "Lion of Judah."

RISE, glorious Conqueror, rise
Into Thy native skies,—
  Assume Thy right;
And where in many a fold
The clouds are backward rolled—
Pass through those gates of gold,
  And reign in light!

2 Lion of Judah—Hail!
And let Thy name prevail
  From age to age;
Lord of the rolling years!
Claim for Thine own the spheres,
For Thou hast bought with tears
  Thy heritage.

3 And then was heard afar
Star answering to star—
  "Lo! these have come,
Followers of Him who gave
His life their lives to save;
And now their palms they wave,
  Brought safely home."

           M. BRIDGES.

ARMSTRONG. 8s, 7s. D. Arr. by EMMELAR.

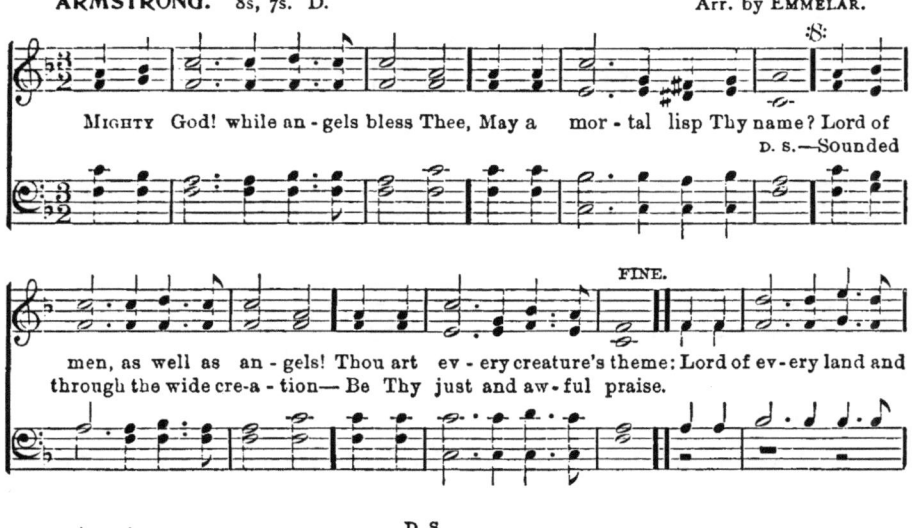

Mighty God! while an-gels bless Thee, May a mor-tal lisp Thy name? Lord of
D. S.—Sounded

men, as well as an-gels! Thou art ev-ery creature's theme: Lord of ev-ery land and
through the wide cre-a-tion— Be Thy just and aw-ful praise.

na-tion! Ancient of e-ternal days!

29 Christ is God.

MIGHTY God! while angels bless Thee,
 May a mortal lisp Thy name?
Lord of men, as well as angels!
 Thou art every creature's theme:
Lord of every land and nation!
 Ancient of eternal days!
Sounded through the wide creation—
 Be Thy just and awful praise.

2 For the grandeur of Thy nature,—
 Grand, beyond a seraph's thought;
For the wonders of creation,
 Works with skill and kindness wrought;

For Thy providence, that governs
 Through Thine empire's wide domain,
Wings an angel, guides a sparrow;—
 Blessèd be Thy gentle reign.
 ANON

30 Holiness.

LORD, Thy glory fills the heaven;
 Earth is with its fullness stored;
Unto Thee be glory given,
 Holy, holy, holy Lord!
Heaven is still with anthems ringing;
 Earth takes up the angels' cry,
Holy, holy, holy, singing,
 Lord of hosts, Thou Lord most high.

2 Lord, Thy glory fills the heaven;
 Earth is with its fullness stored;
Unto Thee be glory given,
 Holy, holy, holy Lord!
Thus Thy glorious name confessing,
 We adopt the angels' cry,
Holy, holy, holy, blessing
 Thee, the Lord our God most high!
 RICHARD MANT.

REPOSE.   7s. 61.   J. P. HOLBROOK, arr.

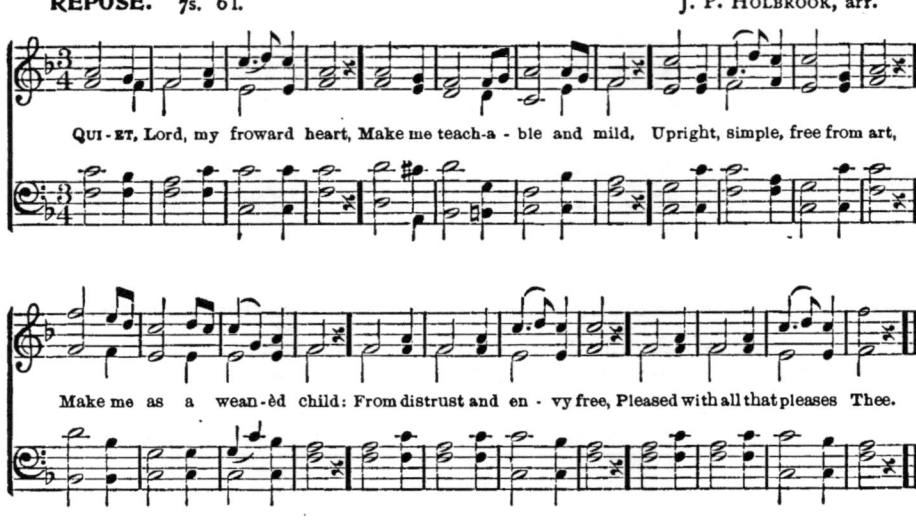

Qui - ET, Lord, my froward heart, Make me teach-a - ble and mild, Upright, simple, free from art,

Make me as a wean-èd child: From distrust and en - vy free, Pleased with all that pleases Thee.

31   Psalm 131.

QUIET, Lord, my froward heart,
  Make me teachable and mild,
Upright, simple, free from art,
  Make me as a weanèd child:
From distrust and envy free,
Pleased with all that pleases Thee.

2 What Thou shalt to-day provide,
  Let me as a child receive;
What to-morrow may betide,
  Calmly to Thy wisdom leave:
'T is enough that Thou wilt care;
Why should I the burden bear?

3 As a little child relies
  On a care beyond his own,
Knows he's neither strong nor wise,
  Fears to stir a step alone;—
Let me thus with Thee abide,
As my Father, Guard, and Guide.

           JOHN NEWTON.

32   Gratitude.

FOR the beauty of the earth,
  For the glory of the skies,
For the love which from our birth
  Over and around us lies:
Lord of all, to Thee we raise
This our grateful psalm of praise.

2 For the wonder of each hour
  Of the day and of the night;
Hill and vale, and tree and flower,
  Sun and moon, and stars of light;
Lord of all, to Thee we raise
This our grateful psalm of praise.

3 For the joy of human love,
  Brother, sister, parent, child;
Friends on earth, and friends above,
  Pleasures pure and undefiled;
Lord of all, to Thee we raise
This our grateful psalm of praise.

           ANON.

RATHBUN.   8s, 7s.   I. CONKEY.

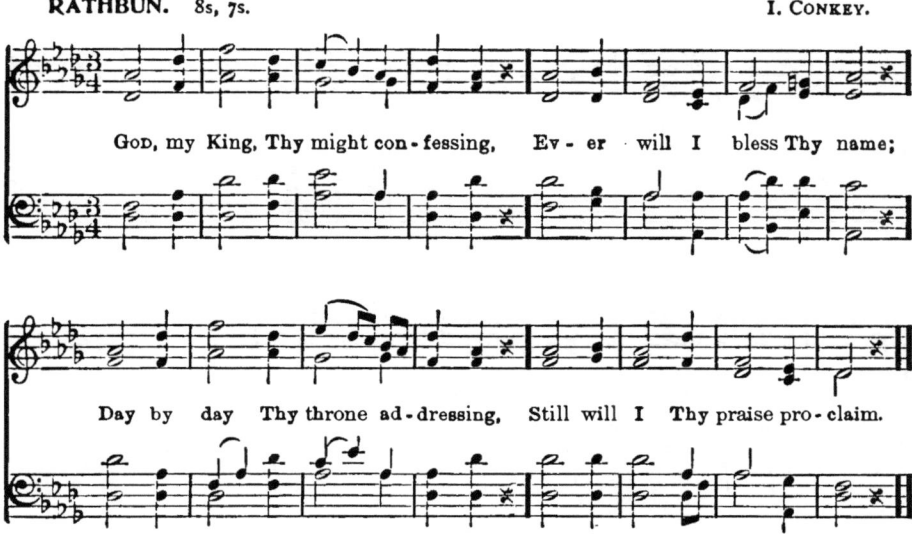

GOD, my King, Thy might con-fessing, Ev-er will I bless Thy name;

Day by day Thy throne ad-dressing, Still will I Thy praise pro-claim.

33   Divine Perfections.

GOD, my King, Thy might confessing,
  Ever will I bless Thy name;
Day by day Thy throne addressing,
  Still will I Thy praise proclaim.

2 Nor shall fail from memory's treasure,
  Works by love and mercy wrought—
Works of love surpassing measure,
  Works of mercy passing thought.

3 Full of kindness and compassion,
  Slow of anger, vast in love,
God is good to all creation;
  All His works His goodness prove.

4 All Thy works, O Lord, shall bless Thee,
  Thee shall all Thy saints adore;
King supreme shall they confess Thee,
  And proclaim Thy sovereign power.
                              RICHARD MANT.

34   Wisdom and Love.

GOD is love; His mercy brightens
  All the path in which we rove;
Bliss He wakes and woe He lightens;
  God is wisdom, God is love.

2 Chance and change are busy ever;
  Man decays, and ages move;
But His mercy waneth never;
  God is wisdom, God is love.

3 Ev'n the hour that darkest seemeth,
  Will His changeless goodness prove;
From the gloom His brightness streameth;
  God is wisdom, God is love.

4 He with earthly cares entwineth
  Hope and comfort from above;
Everywhere His glory shineth;
  God is wisdom, God is love.
                              JOHN BOWRING.

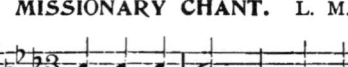

MISSIONARY CHANT. L. M.   CHARLES ZEUNER.

A-WAKE, our souls! a - way, our fears! Let ev-ery trem-bling thought be gone;

A-wake, and run the heav'nly race, And put a cheer-ful cour-age on!

35   Isaiah 40 : 28-31.

AWAKE, our souls! away, our fears!
  Let every trembling thought be gone;
Awake, and run the heavenly race,
  And put a cheerful courage on!

2 True, 'tis a straight and thorny road,
  And mortal spirits tire and faint;
But they forget the mighty God,
  Who feeds the strength of every saint—

3 The mighty God, whose matchless power
  Is ever new and ever young,
And firm endures, while endless years
  Their everlasting circles run.

4 Swift as an eagle cuts the air,
  We'll mount aloft to Thine abode;
On wings of love our souls shall fly,
  Nor tire amid the heavenly road!
                              ISAAC WATTS.

36   National Privileges.

O GOD, beneath Thy guiding hand,
  Our exiled fathers crossed the sea,
And when they trod the wintry strand,
  With prayer and psalm they worshiped
    Thee.

2 Thou heardst, well pleased, the song,
    the prayer—
  Thy blessing came; and still its power
Shall onward through all ages bear
  The memory of that holy hour.

3 What change! through pathless wilds
    no more
  The fierce and naked savage roams:
Sweet praise, along the cultured shore,
  Breaks from ten thousand happy homes.

4 And here Thy name, O God of love,
  Their children's children shall adore,
Till these eternal hills remove,
  And spring adorns the earth no more.
                          LEONARD BACON.

BENEVENTO. 7s. D.   S. WEBBE.

PRAISE to God, im - mor-tal praise, For the love that crowns our days! Bounteous Source of

D. S.—For the fruits in

ev - ery joy, Let Thy praise our tongues em-ploy.   For the bless-ings of the field,
full sup-ply, Ripen'd 'neath the sum-mer sky;—

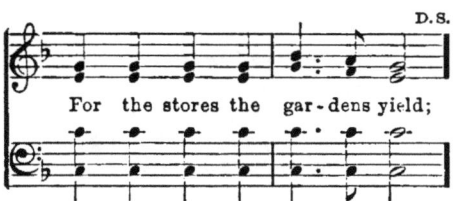

For the stores the gar - dens yield;

37   Thanksgiving.

PRAISE to God, immortal praise,
For the love that crowns our days!
Bounteous Source of every joy,
Let Thy praise our tongues employ.
For the blessings of the field,
For the stores the gardens yield;
For the fruits in full supply,
Ripened 'neath the summer sky;—

2 All that spring with bounteous hand
Scatters o'er the smiling land;
All that liberal autumn pours
From her rich, o'erflowing stores;

These to Thee, my God, we owe,
Source whence all our blessings flow;
And for these my soul shall raise
Grateful vows and solemn praise.
MRS. ANNA L. BARBAULD.

38   Independence Day.

SWELL the anthem, raise the song;
Praises to our God belong;
Saints and angels join to sing
Praises to the heavenly King.
Blessings from His liberal hand
Flow around this happy land:
Kept by Him, no foes annoy;
Peace and freedom we enjoy.

2 Here, beneath a virtuous sway,
May we cheerfully obey;
Never feel oppression's rod,
Ever own and worship God.
Hark! the voice of nature sings
Praises to the King of kings;
Let us join the choral song,
And the grateful notes prolong.
NATHAN STRONG.

SPANISH HYMN.   7s. 6 l.   Spanish Hymn.

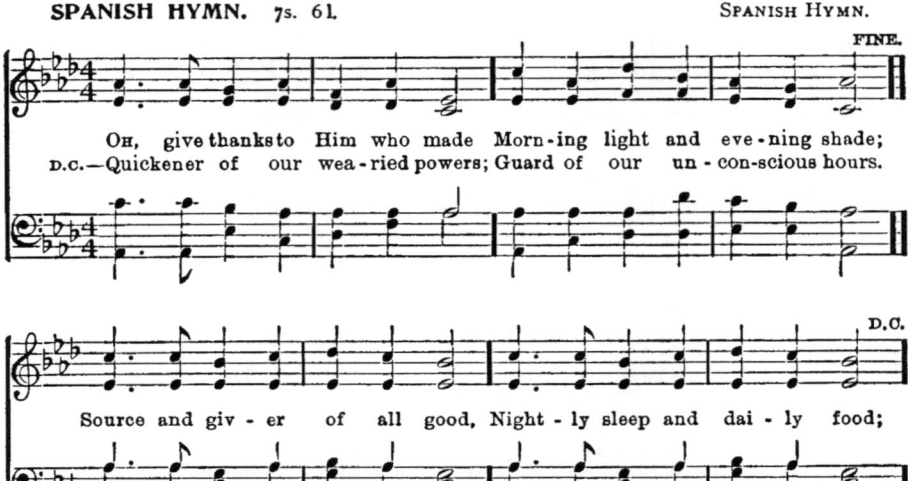

Oh, give thanks to Him who made Morn-ing light and eve-ning shade;
D.C.—Quickener of our wea-ried powers; Guard of our un-con-scious hours.

Source and giv-er of all good, Night-ly sleep and dai-ly food;

39   Nature's King.

Oh, give thanks to Him who made
Morning light and evening shade;
Source and giver of all good,
Nightly sleep and daily food;
Quickener of our wearied powers;
Guard of our unconscious hours.

2 Oh, give thanks to nature's King,
Who made every breathing thing:
His, our warm and sentient frame,
His, the mind's immortal flame.
Oh, how close the ties that bind
Spirits to the Eternal Mind!

3 Oh, give thanks with heart and lip,
For we are His workmanship;
And all creatures are His care:
Not a bird that cleaves the air
Falls unnoticed; but who can
Speak the Father's love to man?

JOSIAH CONDER.

40   "Give us Thy peace."

LORD of mercy and of might,
God and Father of us all,
Lord of day, and Lord of night,
Listen to our solemn call:
Listen, whilst to Thee we raise
Songs of prayer and songs of praise.

2 Shed within our hearts, oh, shed
Thine own Spirit's living flame—
Love for all whom Thou hast made,
Love for all who love Thy name:
Young and old together bless,
Clothe our souls with righteousness.

3 Father, give to us Thy peace:
May our life on earth be blest;
When our trials here shall cease,
May we enter into rest,—
Rest within our home above,
Thee to praise, and Thee to love.

REGINALD HEBER.

ANVERN. L. M.

Arr. by L. Mason.

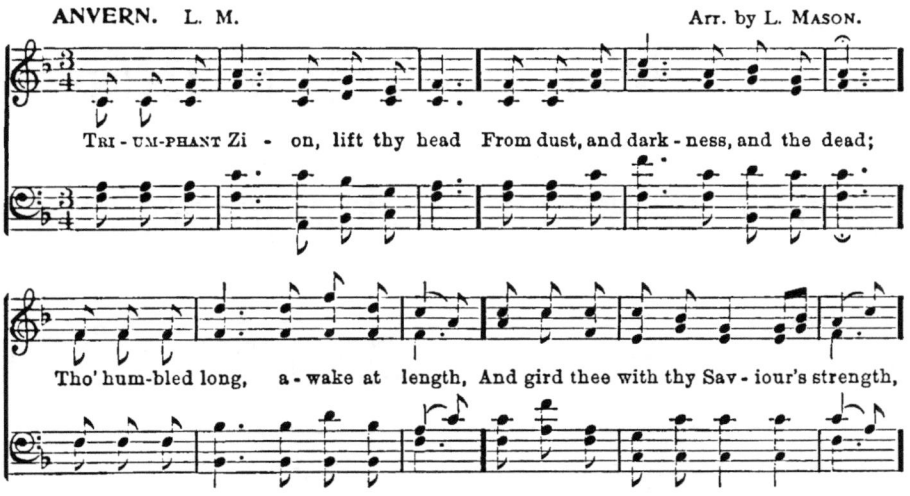

Tri - um-phant Zi - on, lift thy head From dust, and dark - ness, and the dead;

Tho' hum-bled long, a - wake at length, And gird thee with thy Sav - iour's strength,

And gird thee with thy Saviour's strength.

41   " Triumphant Zion."

TRIUMPHANT Zion, lift thy head
From dust, and darkness, and the dead;
Though humbled long, awake at length,
And gird thee with thy Saviour's strength.

2 Put all thy beauteous garments on,
And let thy various charms be known;
The world thy glories shall confess,
Decked in the robes of righteousness.

3 No more shall foes unclean invade,
And fill thy hallowed walls with dread;
No more shall hell's insulting host
Their victory and thy sorrows boast.

4 God, from on high, thy groans will
His hand thy ruins shall repair;   [hear;
Nor will thy watchful Monarch cease
To guard thee in eternal peace.

PHILIP DODDRIDGE.

42   " Eye hath not seen."

Now let our souls, on wings sublime,
Rise from the vanities of time,
Draw back the parting vail, and see
The glories of eternity.

2 Born by a new celestial birth,
Why should we grovel here on earth?
Why grasp at transitory toys,
So near to heaven's eternal joys?

3 Welcome, sweet hour of full discharge!
That sets our longing souls at large,
Unbinds our chains, breaks up our cell,
And gives us with our God to dwell.

4 To dwell with God—to feel His love,
Is the full heaven enjoyed above;
And the sweet expectation now
Is the young dawn of heaven below.

THOMAS GIBBONS.

SEGUR.   8s, 7s. 4s.   J. P. HOLBROOK.

GUIDE me, O Thou great Jeho-vah, Pil-grim thro' this barren land;   I am weak, but Thou art mighty;

Hold me with Thy powerful hand; Bread of beav-en, Bread of beav-en, Feed me till I want no more.

43   Guidance.

GUIDE me, O Thou great Jehovah,
  Pilgrim through this barren land;
I am weak, but Thou art mighty;
  Hold me with Thy powerful hand;
    Bread of heaven,
    Feed me till I want no more.

2 Open Thou the crystal fountain
  Whence the healing streams do flow;
Let the fiery, cloudy pillar
  Lead me all my journey through;
    Strong Deliverer,
    Be Thou still my Strength and Shield.

3 When I tread the verge of Jordan,
  Bid my anxious fears subside;
Death of death! and hell's Destruction!
  Land me safe on Canaan's side;
    Songs of praises
    I will ever give to Thee.
                    WILLIAM WILLIAMS.

44   "Hallelujah."

HALLELUJAH! best and sweetest
  Of the hymns of praise above;
Hallelujah! Thou repeatest,
  Angel Host, these notes of love;
    This ye utter,
    While your golden harps ye move.

2 Hallelujah! Church Victorious,
  Join the concert of the sky;
Hallelujah! bright and glorious,
  Lift, ye Saints, this strain on high;
    We, poor exiles,
    Join not yet your melody.

3 But our earnest supplication,
  Holy God, we raise to Thee;
Visit us with Thy salvation,
  Make us all Thy joys to see.
    Hallelujah!
    Ours at length this strain shall be.
                    JOHN CHANDLER, tr.

ST. ALBAN. L. M.   ST. ALBAN'S TUNE-BOOK.

High in the heav'ns, e - ter - nal God! Thy good-ness in full glo - ry shines;

Thy truth shall break thro' ev - ery cloud That vails and dark - ens Thy de - signs.

45   Psalm 36.

HIGH in the heavens, eternal God!
  Thy goodness in full glory shines;
Thy truth shall break through every cloud
  That vails and darkens Thy designs.

2 For ever firm Thy justice stands,
  As mountains their foundations keep:
Wise are the wonders of Thy hands;
  Thy judgments are a mighty deep.

3 From the provisions of Thy house
  We shall be fed with sweet repast;
There, mercy like a river flows,
  And brings salvation to our taste.

4 Life, like a fountain rich and free,
  Springs from the presence of my Lord;
And in Thy light our souls shall see
  The glories promised in Thy word.
                    ISAAC WATTS.

46   Home Missions.

LOOK from Thy sphere of endless day,
  O God of mercy and of might!
In pity look on those who stray,
  Benighted in this land of light.

2 In peopled vale, in lonely glen,
  In crowded mart, by stream or sea,
How many of the sons of men
  Hear not the message sent from Thee!

3 Send forth Thy heralds, Lord, to call
  The thoughtless young, the hardened old,
A scattered, homeless flock, till all
  Be gathered to Thy peaceful fold.

4 Then all these wastes, a dreary scene,
  That makes us sadden as we gaze,
Shall grow with living waters green,
  And lift to heaven the voice of praise.
              WILLIAM C. BRYANT.

WARWICK. C. M.

S. STANLEY.

The Lord of glo-ry is my light, And my sal-va-tion too;

God is my strength,—nor will I fear What all my foes can do.

47   Psalm 27.

The Lord of glory is my light,
  And my salvation too;
God is my strength,—nor will I fear
  What all my foes can do.

2 One privilege my heart desires,—
  Oh, grant me an abode
Among the churches of Thy saints,—
  The temples of my God.

3 There shall I offer my requests,
  And see Thy beauty still;
Shall hear Thy messages of love,
  And there inquire Thy will.

4 When troubles rise, and storms appear,
  There may His children hide;
God has a strong pavilion, where
  He makes my soul abide.

ISAAC WATTS.

48   The Mercy-seat.

Dear Father, to Thy mercy-seat
  My soul for shelter flies:
'T is here I find a safe retreat
  When storms and tempests rise.

2 My cheerful hope can never die,
  If Thou, my God, art near;
Thy grace can raise my comforts high,
  And banish every fear.

3 My great Protector and my Lord,
  Thy constant aid impart;
Oh, let Thy kind, Thy gracious word
  Sustain my trembling heart!

4 Oh, never let my soul remove
  From this divine retreat!
Still let me trust Thy power and love,
  And dwell beneath Thy feet.

ANNE STEELE.

SESSIONS. L. M.

L. O. EMERSON.

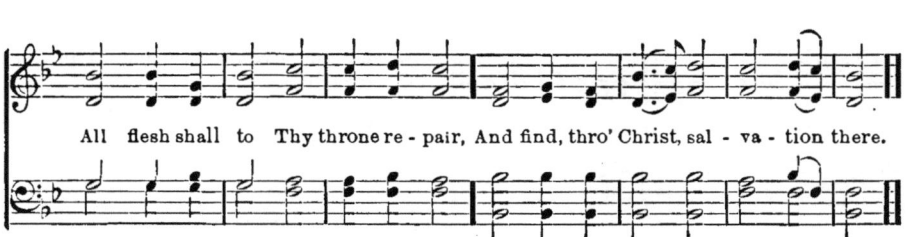

PRAISE, Lord, for Thee in Zi-on waits; Pray'r shall be-siege Thy tem-ple gates;

All flesh shall to Thy throne re-pair, And find, thro' Christ, sal-va-tion there.

49   Psalm 65.

PRAISE, Lord, for Thee in Zion waits;
Prayer shall besiege Thy temple gates;
All flesh shall to Thy throne repair,
And find, through Christ, salvation there.

2 How blest Thy saints! how safely led!
How surely kept! how richly fed!
Saviour of all in earth and sea,
How happy they who rest in Thee!

3 Thy hand sets fast the mighty hills,
Thy voice the troubled ocean stills;
Evening and morning hymn Thy praise,
And earth Thy bounty wide displays.

4 The year is with Thy goodness crowned;
Thy clouds drop wealth the world around;
Through Thee the deserts laugh and sing,
And nature smiles and owns her King.

HENRY F. LYTE.

50   A Joyful Song.

SING to the Lord a joyful song;
  Lift up your hearts, your voices raise;
To us His gracious gifts belong,
  To Him our songs of love and praise.

2 For life and love, for rest and food,
  For daily help and nightly care,
Sing to the Lord, for He is good,
  And praise His name, for it is fair:—

3 For strength to those who on Him wait,
  His truth to prove, His will to do,
Praise ye our God, for He is great,
  Trust in His name, for it is true:—

4 For joys untold that daily move
  Round those who love His sweet employ,
Sing to our God, for He is love,
  Exalt His name, for it is joy.

J. S. B. MONSELL.

HENLEY.   11s, 10s.   LOWELL MASON.

FA-THER! in Thy mys-te-rious presence kneeling, Fain would our souls feel all Thy kindling love;
D.S.—Of trust, and strength, and calmness from above.

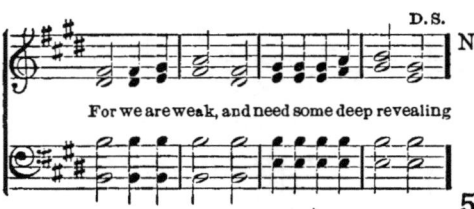

For we are weak, and need some deep revealing

51   "Trust, strength, calmness."

FATHER! in Thy mysterious presence kneeling,
  Fain would our souls feel all Thy kindling love;
For we are weak, and need some deep revealing
  Of trust, and strength, and calmness from above.

2 Lord! we have wandered forth through doubt and sorrow,
  And Thou hast made each step an onward one;
And we will ever trust each unknown morrow;
  Thou wilt sustain us till its work is done.

3 Now, Father! now in Thy dear presence kneeling,
  Our spirits yearn to feel Thy kindling love;

Now make us strong; we need Thy deep revealing
  Of trust, and strength, and calmness from above.

SAMUEL JOHNSON.

52   The Sabbath of the Sea.

WHEN winds are raging o'er the upper ocean,
  And billows wild contend with angry roar,
'Tis said, far down, beneath the wild commotion,
  That peaceful stillness reigneth evermore.

2 Far, far beneath, the noise of tempests dieth,
  And silver waves chime ever peacefully,
And no rude storm, how fierce soe'er it flieth,
  Disturbs the Sabbath of that deeper sea.

3 Far, far away, the roar of passion dieth,
  And loving thoughts rise kind and peacefully,
And no rude storm, how fierce soe'er it flieth,
  Disturbs the soul that dwells, O Lord, in Thee.

Mrs. H. B. STOWE.

YORK. C. M. SCOTCH PSALTER.

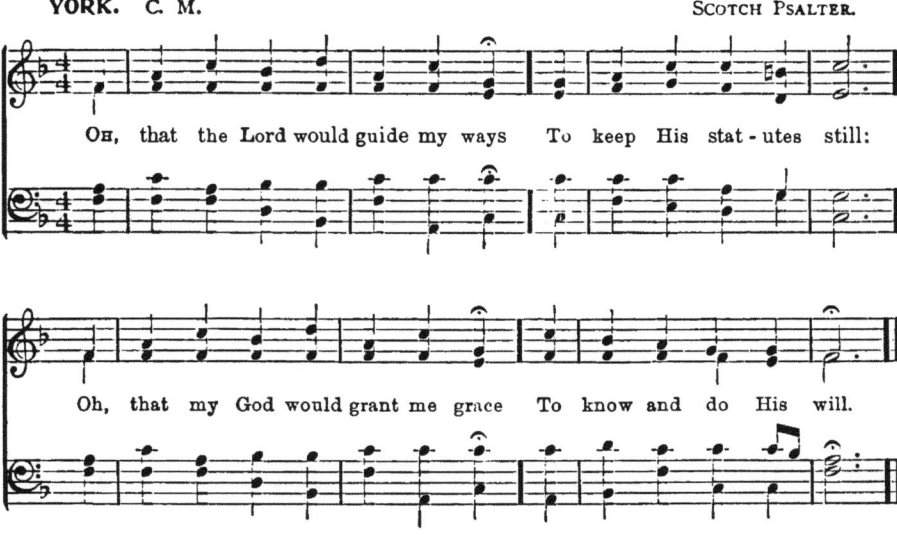

Oh, that the Lord would guide my ways To keep His stat-utes still:

Oh, that my God would grant me grace To know and do His will.

53 Psalm 119.

OH, that the Lord would guide my ways
 To keep His statutes still:
Oh, that my God would grant me grace
 To know and do His will.

2 Oh, send Thy Spirit down, to write
 Thy law upon my heart;
Nor let my tongue indulge deceit,
 Or act the liar's part.

3 Order my footsteps by Thy word,
 And make my heart sincere;
Let sin have no dominion, Lord!
 But keep my conscience clear.

4 Make me to walk in Thy commands—
 'Tis a delightful road;
Nor let my head, or heart, or hands,
 Offend against my God.

ISAAC WATTS.

54 Power.

THE Lord, our God, is full of might,
 The winds obey His will;
He speaks,—and, in His heavenly height,
 The rolling sun stands still.

2 Rebel, ye waves, and o'er the land
 With threatening aspect roar;
The Lord uplifts His awful hand,
 And chains you to the shore.

3 His voice sublime is heard afar,
 In distant peals it dies;
He yokes the whirlwind to His car,
 And sweeps the howling skies.

4 Ye nations, bend—in reverence bend
 Ye monarchs, wait His nod,
And bid the choral song ascend
 To celebrate your God.

HENRY KIRKE WHITE.

HEBRON. L. M.   Lowell Mason.

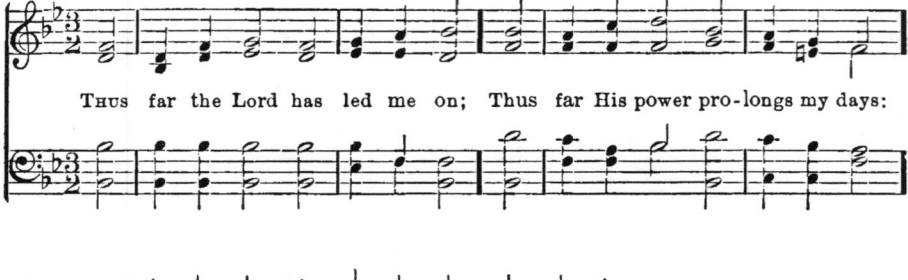

Thus far the Lord has led me on; Thus far His power pro-longs my days:

And ev-ery eve-ning shall make known Some fresh me-mo-rial of His grace.

55   Evening.

Thus far the Lord has led me on;
  Thus far His power prolongs my days;
And every evening shall make known
  Some fresh memorial of His grace.

2 Much of my time has run to waste,
  And I, perhaps, am near my home,
But He forgives my follies past,
  And gives me strength for days to come.

3 I lay my body down to sleep;
  Peace is the pillow for my head;
While well-appointed angels keep
  Their watchful stations round my bed.

4 Thus when the night of death shall come,
  My flesh shall rest beneath the ground,
And wait Thy voice to break my tomb,
  With sweet salvation in the sound.

                            Isaac Watts.

56   God our Light.

All holy, everliving One!
  With uncreated splendor bright!
Darkness may blot from heaven the sun,
  Thou art my everlasting light.

2 Let every star withhold its ray;
  Clouds hide the earth and sky from sight;
Fearless I still pursue my way
  Toward Thee, my everlasting light.

3 Thou art the only source of day;
  Forgetting Thee alone is night;
All things for which we hope or pray
  Flow from Thine everlasting light.

4 Still nearer Thee my soul would rise;
  Thus she attains her highest flight,
And, as the eagle sunward flies,
  Seeks Thee, her everlasting light.

                            Thomas Hill.

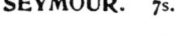

SEYMOUR. 7s.   Arr. fr. Von Weber.

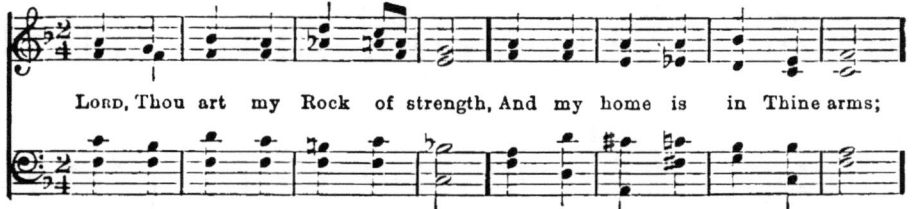

Lord, Thou art my Rock of strength, And my home is in Thine arms;

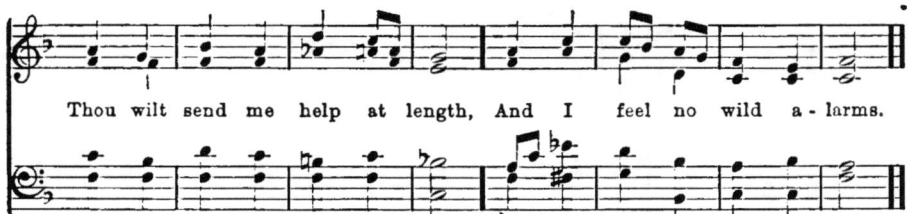

Thou wilt send me help at length, And I feel no wild a-larms.

57   Strong in Trust.

Lord, Thou art my Rock of strength,
  And my home is in Thine arms;
Thou wilt send me help at length,
  And I feel no wild alarms.

2 When my trials tarry long,
  Unto Thee I look and wait,
Knowing none, though keen and strong,
  Can my trust in Thee abate.

3 And this faith I long have nursed
  Comes alone, O God, from Thee;
Thou my heart didst open first,
  Thou didst set this hope in me.

4 Let Thy mercy's wings be spread
  O'er me, keep me close to Thee;
In the peace Thy love doth shed
  Let me dwell eternally.

                    C. Winkworth. tr.

58   "Thine for ever."

Thine for ever! God of love,
Hear us from Thy throne above!
Thine for ever may we be,
Here and in eternity!

2 Thine for ever! oh, how blest
They who find in Thee their rest!
Saviour, Guardian, heavenly Friend,
Oh, defend us to the end!

3 Thine for ever! Saviour, keep
These Thy frail and trembling sheep;
Safe alone beneath Thy care,
Let us all Thy goodness share.

4 Thine for ever! Thou our Guide,—
All our wants by Thee supplied,—
All our sins by Thee forgiven,—
Lead us, Lord, from earth to heaven!
                    Mrs. Mary F. Maude.

CHRISTMAS. C. M.   Arr. fr. HANDEL.

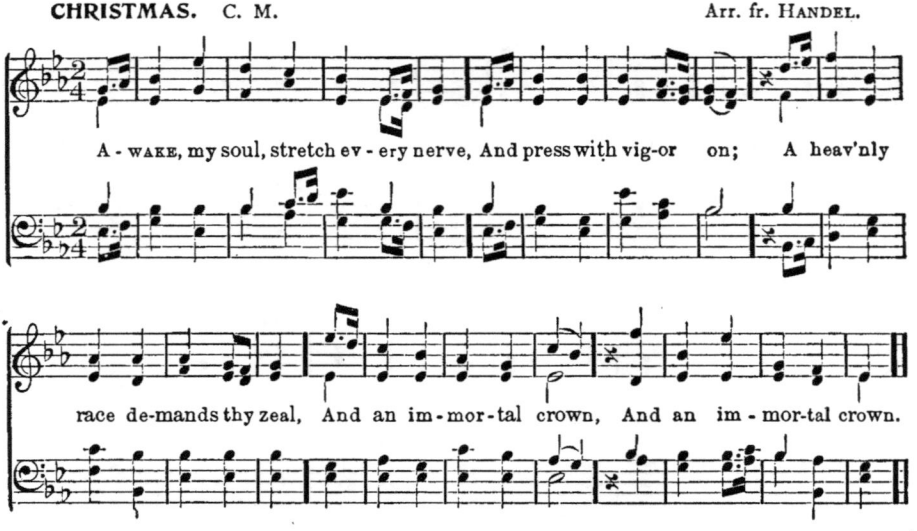

A - wake, my soul, stretch ev - ery nerve, And press with vig-or on; A heav'nly

race de-mands thy zeal, And an im - mor-tal crown, And an im - mor-tal crown.

59   The Race.

AWAKE, my soul, stretch every nerve,
  And press with vigor on;
A heavenly race demands thy zeal,
  And an immortal crown.

2 A cloud of witnesses around
  Hold thee in full survey;
Forget the steps already trod,
  And onward urge thy way.

3 'T is God's all-animating voice,
  That calls thee from on high,
'T is His own hand presents the prize
  To thine aspiring eye.

4 Blest Saviour, introduced by Thee,
  Have I my race begun;
And, crowned with victory, at Thy feet
  I 'll lay my honors down.
                    PHILIP DODDRIDGE.

60   Psalm 23.

THE Lord's my shepherd, I 'll not want:
  He makes me down to lie

In pastures green; He leadeth me
  The quiet waters by.

2 My soul He doth restore again;
  And me to walk doth make
Within the paths of righteousness,
  Ev'n for His own name's sake.

3 Yea, though I walk in death's dark vale,
  Yet will I fear no ill;
For Thou art with me, and Thy rod
  And staff me comfort still.

4 My table Thou hast furnishèd
  In presence of my foes;
My head Thou dost with oil anoint,
  And my cup overflows.

5 Goodness and mercy, all my life,
  Shall surely follow me;
And in God's house for evermore
  My dwelling-place shall be.
                    FRANCIS ROUS.

WIMBORNE. L. M.   J. WHITAKER.

Come, O Cre-a-tor, Spir-it blest! And in our souls take up Thy rest;

Come, with Thy grace, and heav'n-ly aid, To fill the hearts which Thou hast made.

61   "Veni, Creator."

COME, O Creator, Spirit blest!
And in our souls take up Thy rest;
Come, with Thy grace, and heavenly aid,
To fill the hearts which Thou hast made.

2 Great Comforter! to Thee we cry;
O highest gift of God most high!
O fount of life! O fire of love!
Send sweet anointing from above!

3 Kindle our senses from above,
And make our hearts o'erflow with love;
With patience firm and virtue high,
The weakness of our flesh supply.

4 Far from us drive the foe we dread,
And grant us Thy true peace instead;
So shall we not, with Thee for guide,
Turn from the path of life aside.
                         EDWARD CASWALL, tr.

62   "The Book Unfold."

COME, blessèd Spirit! source of light!
Whose power and grace are unconfined;
Dispel the gloomy shades of night—
The thicker darkness of the mind.

2 To mine illumined eyes, display
The glorious truths Thy word reveals;
Cause me to run the heavenly way,
Thy book unfold, and loose the seals.

3 Thine inward teachings make me know
The mysteries of redeeming love,
The vanity of things below,
And excellence of things above.

4 While through this dubious maze I stray,
Spread, like the sun, Thy beams abroad,
To show the dangers of the way,
And guide my feeble steps to God.
                         BENJAMIN BEDDOME.

LOVE DIVINE.   8s, 7s. D.   JOHN ZUNDEL.

Ho-ly Fa-ther, Thou hast taught me I should live to Thee a-lone; Year by year Thy hand hath brought me
                                              D. s.—Still Thine arm has been around me,

On thro' dan-gers oft un-known. When I wander'd, Thou hast found me; When I doubted, sent me light;
All my paths were in Thy sight.

63   "Keep me ever."

Holy Father, Thou hast taught me
  I should live to Thee alone;
Year by year Thy hand hath brought me
  On through dangers oft unknown.
When I wandered, Thou hast found me;
  When I doubted, sent me light;
Still Thine arm has been around me,
  All my paths were in Thy sight.

2 In the world will foes assail me,
  Craftier, stronger far than I;
And the strife may never fail me,
  Well I know, before I die.
Therefore, Lord, I come believing
  Thou canst give the power I need;
Through the prayer of faith receiving
  Strength—the Spirit's strength, indeed.

3 I would trust in Thy protection,
  Wholly rest upon Thine arm;
Follow wholly Thy direction,
  Thou, mine only guard from harm!

Keep me from mine own undoing,
  Help me turn to Thee when tried,
Still my footsteps, Father, viewing,
  Keep me ever at Thy side.
                         JOHN M. NEALE.

64   "What thy hand findeth."

If you cannot on the ocean
  Sail among the swiftest fleet,
Rocking on the highest billows,
  Laughing at the storms you meet,
You can stand among the sailors,
  Anchored yet within the bay,
You can lend a hand to help them,
  As they launch their boat away.

2 If you are too weak to journey
  Up the mountain steep and high,
You can stand within the valley,
  While the multitude go by;
You can chant in happy measure,
  As they slowly pass along;
Though they may forget the singer,
  They will not forget the song.

3 If you have not gold and silver
 Ever ready to command;
If you cannot toward the needy
 Reach an ever open hand,

You can visit the afflicted,
 O'er the erring you can weep;
You can be a true disciple
 Sitting at the Saviour's feet.
E. H. Gates.

HUMMEL.   C. M.   C. Zeuner.

Oh, for a thou-sand tongues to sing My dear Re-deem-er's praise! The glo-ries of my God and King, The tri-umphs of His grace!

65   Thanks for Victory.

OH, for a thousand tougues to sing
 My dear Redeemer's praise!
The glories of my God and King,
 The triumphs of His grace!

2 My gracious Master and my God!
 Assist me to proclaim,
To spread through all the earth abroad
 The honors of Thy name.

3 Jesus—the name that calms my fears,
 That bids my sorrows cease;
'Tis music to my ravished ears;
 'Tis life, and health, and peace.

4 He breaks the power of canceled sin,
 He sets the prisoner free;
His blood can make the foulest clean;
 His blood availed for me.

5 Let us obey, we then shall know,
 Shall feel our sins forgiven;

Anticipate our heaven below,
 And own that love is heaven.
Charles Wesley.

66   Martyr-faith.

GLORY to God! whose witness-train,
 Those heroes bold in faith,
Could smile on poverty and pain,
 And triumph ev'n in death.

2 Oh, may that faith our hearts sustain,
 Wherein they fearless stood,
When, in the power of cruel men,
 They poured their willing blood.

3 God whom we serve, our God, can save,
 Can damp the scorching flame,
Can build an ark, can smooth the wave,
 For such as love His name.

4 Lord! if Thine arm support us still
 With its eternal strength,
We shall o'ercome the mightiest ill,
 And conquerors prove at length.
Tr. fr. Zinzendorf.

LEIGHTON. S. M.   H. W. GREATOREX.

A - rise, ye saints, a - rise! The Lord our Lead-er is;

The foe be - fore His ban - ner flies, And vic - to - ry is His.

67   Psalm 60.

ARISE, ye saints, arise!
  The Lord our Leader is;
The foe before His banner flies,
  And victory is His.

2 We follow Thee, our Guide,
  Our Saviour, and our King!
We follow Thee, through grace supplied
  From heaven's eternal spring.

3 We soon shall see the day
  When all our toils shall cease;
When we shall cast our arms away,
  And dwell in endless peace.

4 This hope supports us here;
  It makes our burdens light;
'Twill serve our drooping hearts to cheer,
  Till faith shall end in sight.
                        THOMAS KELLY.

68   Christian Pilgrims.

THE people of the Lord
  Are on their way to heaven;
There they obtain their great reward;
  The prize will there be given.

2 'Tis conflict here below;
  'Tis triumph there, and peace:
On earth we wrestle with the foe;
  In heaven our conflicts cease.

3 'Tis gloom and darkness here;
  'Tis light and joy above;
There all is pure, and all is clear;
  There all is peace and love.

4 There rest shall follow toil,
  And ease succeed to care:
The victors there divide the spoil;
  They sing and triumph there.
                        THOMAS KELLY.

GROSTETE. L. M. H. W. GREATOREX.

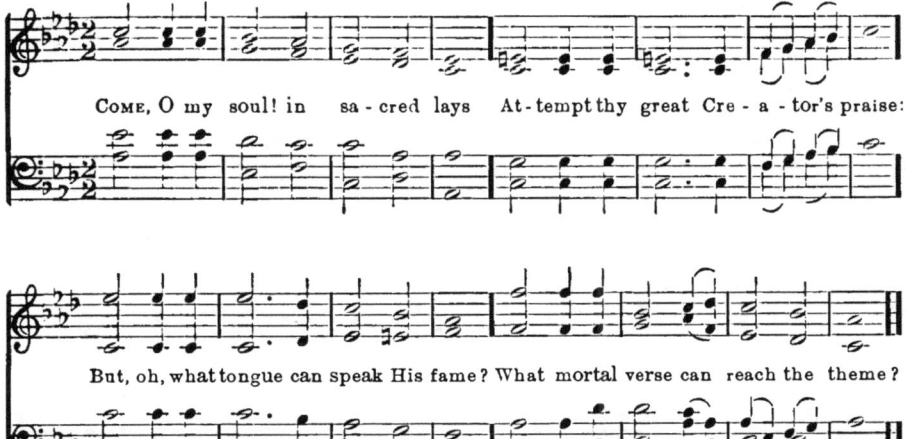

Come, O my soul! in sa - cred lays At-tempt thy great Cre - a - tor's praise:

But, oh, what tongue can speak His fame? What mortal verse can reach the theme?

69   God's Glory.

COME, O my soul! in sacred lays
Attempt thy great Creator's praise:
But, oh, what tongue can speak His fame?
What mortal verse can reach the theme?

2 Enthroned amid the radiant spheres,
He glory like a garment wears;
To form a robe of light divine,
Ten thousand suns around Him shine.

3 In all our Maker's grand designs,
Almighty power with wisdom shines;
His works through all this wondrous frame
Declare the glory of His name.

4 Raised on devotion's lofty wing,
Do thou, my soul, His glories sing;
And let His praise employ thy tongue,
Till listening worlds shall join the song!
THOMAS BLACKLOCK.

70   Psalm 29.

GIVE to the Lord, ye sons of fame,
Give to the Lord renown and power;
Ascribe due honors to His name,
And His eternal might adore.

2 The Lord proclaims His power aloud,
O'er all the ocean and the land;
His voice divides the watery cloud,
And lightnings blaze at His command.

3 The Lord sits Sovereign on the flood;
The Thunderer reigns for ever King;
But makes His church His blest abode,
Where we His awful glories sing.

4 In gentler language, there the Lord
The counsels of His grace imparts;
Amid the raging storm, His word
Speaks peace and courage to our hearts.
ISAAC WATTS.

ANTIOCH.   C. M.   Arr. by L. Mason.

Joy to the world; the Lord is come! Let earth re-ceive her King; { Let ev - ery heart pre - pare Him room,

And heav'n and nature sing, And heav'n and nature sing,............. And heav'n and na-ture sing.

And heav'n and nature sing, And heav'n and nature sing,

71   Psalm 98.

Joy to the world; the Lord is come!
  Let earth receive her King;
Let every heart prepare Him room,
  And heaven and nature sing.

2 Joy to the earth; the Saviour reigns;
  Let men their songs employ;
While fields and floods, rocks, hills and plains,
  Repeat the sounding joy.

3 No more let sins and sorrows grow,
  Nor thorns infest the ground;
He comes to make His blessings flow
  Far as the curse is found.

4 He rules the world with truth and grace,
  And makes the nations prove
The glories of His righteousness,
  And wonders of His love.

Isaac Watts.

72   Psalm 116.

What shall I render to my God,
  For all His kindness shown?
My feet shall visit Thine abode,
  My songs address Thy throne.

2 Among the saints that fill Thine house,
  My offering shall be paid;
There shall my zeal perform the vows,
  My soul in anguish made.

3 How much is mercy Thy delight,
  Thou ever blessèd God!
How dear Thy servants in Thy sight!
  How precious is their blood!

4 How happy all Thy servants are!
  How great Thy grace to me!
My life, which Thou hast made Thy care,
  Lord, I devote to Thee.

Isaac Watts.

CHERITH. C. M. Arr. fr. SPOHR.

As pants the hart for cool - ing streams, When heat - ed in the chase,

So longs my soul, O God, for Thee, And Thy re - fresh - ing grace.

73 Psalm 42.

As pants the hart for cooling streams,
  When heated in the chase,
So longs my soul, O God, for Thee,
  And Thy refreshing grace.

2 For Thee, my God—the living God,
  My thirsty soul doth pine,
Oh, when shall I behold Thy face,
  Thou Majesty divine!

3 Why restless, why cast down, my soul?
  Trust God; who will employ
His aid for thee, and change these sighs
  To thankful hymns of joy.

4 I sigh to think of happier days,
  When Thou, O Lord! wast nigh;
When every heart was tuned to praise,
  And none more blest than I.
               HENRY F. LYTE.

74 Protection.—Psalm 34.

THROUGH all the changing scenes of life,
  In trouble, and in joy,
The praises of my God shall still
  My heart and tongue employ.

2 Oh, magnify the Lord with me,
  With me exalt His name!
When in distress to Him I called,
  He to my rescue came.

3 The hosts of God encamp around
  The dwellings of the just;
Deliverance He affords to all,
  Who on His succor trust.

4 Oh, make but trial of His love;
  Experience will decide,
How blest are they, and only they,
  Who in His truth confide
               TATE AND BRADY.

MIGDOL. L. M.   LOWELL MASON.

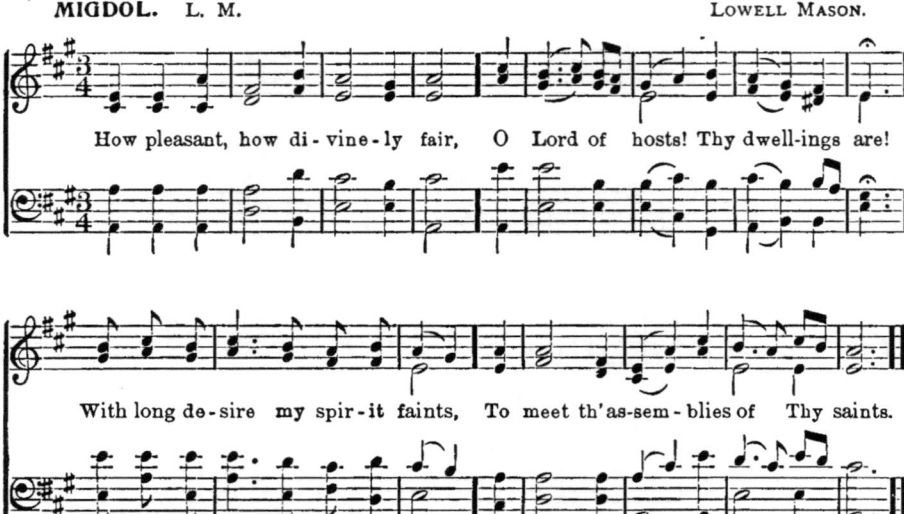

How pleasant, how di-vine-ly fair, O Lord of hosts! Thy dwell-ings are!

With long de-sire my spir-it faints, To meet th'as-sem-blies of Thy saints.

75   Psalm 84.

How pleasant, how divinely fair,
O Lord of hosts! Thy dwellings are!
With long desire my spirit faints,
To meet the assemblies of Thy saints.

2 My flesh would rest in Thine abode,
My panting heart cries out for God;
My God! my King! why should I be
So far from all my joys, and Thee?

3 Blest are the saints who sit on high,
Around Thy throne of majesty;
Thy brightest glories shine above,
And all their work is praise and love.

4 Blest are the souls who find a place
Within the temple of Thy grace;
There they behold Thy gentler rays,
And seek Thy face, and learn Thy praise.
                                    ISAAC WATTS.

76   Psalm 92.

SWEET is the work, my God, my King.
To praise Thy name, give thanks, and sing;
To show Thy love by morning light,
And talk of all Thy truth at night.

2 Sweet is the day of sacred rest;
No mortal cares shall seize my breast;
Oh! may my heart in tune be found,
Like David's harp of solemn sound!

3 My heart shall triumph in my Lord,
And bless His works, and bless His word;
Thy works of grace, how bright they shine!
How deep Thy counsels! how divine!

4 Lord! I shall share a glorious part,
When grace hath well refined my heart,
And fresh supplies of joy are shed,
Like holy oil to cheer my head.
                                    ISAAC WATTS.

BEMERTON. C. M.

H. W. GREATOREX.

Lord! when we bend be - fore Thy throne, And our con - fes - sions pour,

Oh, may we feel the sins we own, And hate what we de - plore.

77   Sincerity.

Lord! when we bend before Thy throne,
  And our confessions pour,
Oh, may we feel the sins we own,
  And hate what we deplore.

2 Our contrite spirits pitying see;
  True penitence impart:
And let a healing ray from Thee
  Beam hope on every heart.

3 When we disclose our wants in prayer,
  May we our wills resign;
Nor let a thought our bosom share,
  Which is not wholly Thine.

4 Let faith each meek petition fill,
  And waft it to the skies;
And teach our heart 't is goodness still
  That grants it or denies.

                Jos. Dacre Carlyle.

78   Psalm 63.

Early, my God, without delay,
  I haste to seek Thy face;
My thirsty spirit faints away,
  Without Thy cheering grace.

2 I've seen Thy glory and Thy power
  Through all Thy temples shine;
My God, repeat that heavenly hour,
  That vision so divine.

3 Not life itself, with all its joys,
  Can my best passions move,
Or raise so high my cheerful voice,
  As Thy forgiving love.

4 Thus, till my last expiring day,
  I'll bless my God and King;
Thus will I lift my hand to pray,
  And tune my lips to sing.

                Isaac Watts.

PETERBORO'. C. M.   R. HARRISON.

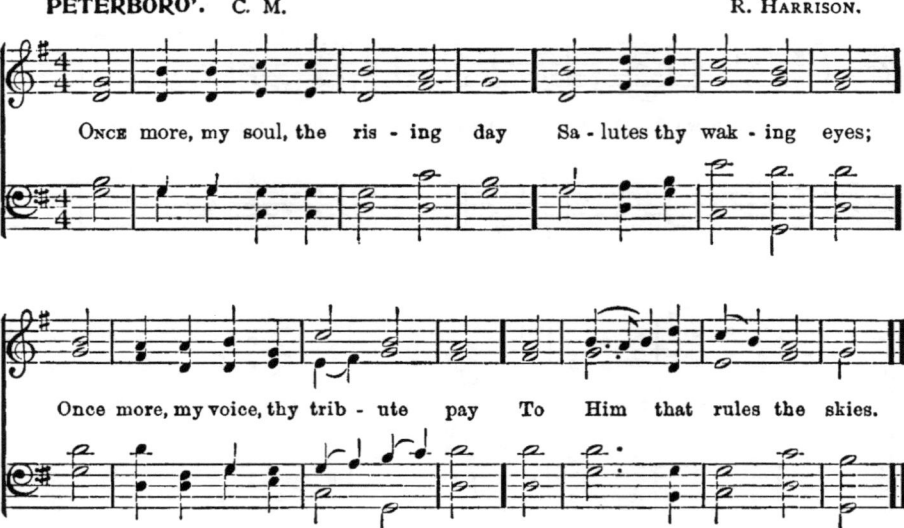

Once more, my soul, the ris - ing day   Sa - lutes thy wak - ing eyes;

Once more, my voice, thy trib - ute   pay   To   Him   that   rules the   skies.

79   "The Rising Day."

Once more, my soul, the rising day
  Salutes thy waking eyes;
Once more, my voice, thy tribute pay
  To Him that rules the skies.

2 Night unto night His name repeats
  The day renews the sound,
Wide as the heaven on which He sits
  To turn the seasons round.

3 'T is He supports my mortal frame;
  My tongue shall speak His praise;
My sins would rouse His wrath to flame,
  And yet His wrath delays.

4 Great God, let all my hours be Thine,
  While I enjoy the light;
Then shall my sun in smiles decline,
  And bring a pleasant night
                          Isaac Watts.

80   Psalm 25 : 14.

Speak to me, Lord, Thyself reveal,
  While here on earth I rove;
Speak to my heart, and let me feel
  The kindling of Thy love.

2 With Thee conversing, I forget
  All time and toil and care;
Labor is rest, and pain is sweet,
  If Thou, my God, art here.

3 Thou callest me to seek Thy face;
  Thy face, O God, I seek,—
Attend the whispers of Thy grace,
  And hear Thee inly speak.

4 Let this my every hour employ,
  Till I Thy glory see,
Enter into my Master's joy,
  And find my heaven in Thee.
                          Charles Wesley.

DARWALL. H. M.

J. DARWALL.

Lord of the worlds a - bove! How pleasant, and how fair, The dwellings of Thy love, Thine earthly

tem-ples are! To Thine a - bode my heart aspires, With warm de-sires to see my God.

81   Psalm 84.

Lord of the worlds above!
  How pleasant, and how fair,
The dwellings of Thy love,
  Thine earthly temples are!
To Thine abode my heart aspires,
With warm desires to see my God.

2 Oh, happy souls who pray,
  Where God appoints to hear!
Oh, happy men who pay
  Their constant service there!
They praise Thee still; and happy they,
Who love the way to Zion's hill.

3 They go from strength to strength,
  Through this dark vale of tears,
Till each arrives at length,
  Till each in heaven appears;
Oh, glorious seat, when God, our King,
Shall thither bring our willing feet!
                 Isaac Watts.

82   Psalm 43.

Now, to Thy sacred house,
  With joy I turn my feet,
Where saints, with morning-vows,
  In full assembly meet:
Thy power divine shall there be shown,
And from Thy throne Thy mercy shine.

2 Oh, send Thy light abroad;
  Thy truth with heavenly ray
Shall lead my soul to God,
  And guide my doubtful way;
I 'll hear Thy word with faith sincere,
And learn to fear and praise the Lord.

3 Now in Thy holy hill,
  Before Thine altar, Lord!
My harp and song shall sound
  The glories of Thy word:
Henceforth, to Thee, O God of grace!
A hymn of praise my life shall be.
             Timothy Dwight.

VIGIL.   S. M.   G. PAISIELLO.

My God! per-mit my tongue This joy, to call Thee mine;

And let my ear-ly cries pre-vail To taste Thy love di-vine.

83   Psalm 63.

My God! permit my tongue
  This joy, to call Thee mine;
And let my early cries prevail
  To taste Thy love divine.

2 My thirsty fainting soul
  Thy mercy doth implore;
Not travelers, in desert lands,
  Can pant for water more.

3 For life, without Thy love,
  No relish can afford;
No joy can be compared to this,—
  To serve and please the Lord.

4 The shadow of Thy wings
  My soul in safety keeps;
I follow where my Father leads,
  And He supports my steps.

                       Isaac Watts.

84   "Be of Good Courage."

Give to the winds thy fears;
  Hope, and be undismayed;
God hears thy sighs and counts thy tears;
  God shall lift up thy head.

2 Through waves, and clouds, and storms,
  He gently clears thy way;
Wait thou His time; so shall this night
  Soon end in joyous day.

3 The battle soon will yield,
  If thou thy part fulfill;
For strong as is the hostile shield,
  Thy sword is stronger still.

4 Thine armor is divine,
  Thy feet with victory shod;
And on thy head shall quickly shine
  The diadem of God.

                       Leonard Swain.

ALVAN. 8s, 7s, 4s.   LOWELL MASON.

{ Come, Thou soul - transform - ing Spir - it,   Bless the sow - er and the seed; }
{ Let   each heart Thy grace in - her - it;   Raise the weak, the hun - gry feed! }

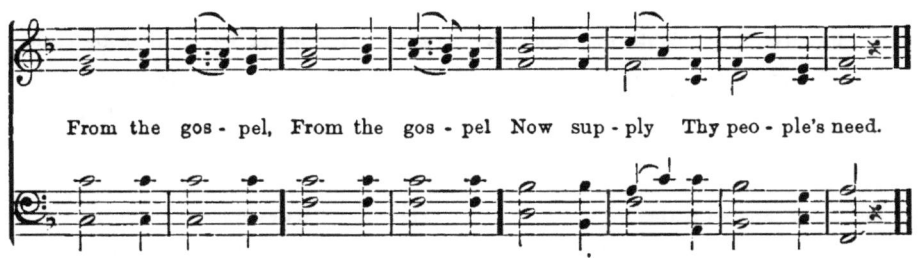

From the gos - pel, From the gos - pel Now sup - ply Thy peo - ple's need.

85   " Bless the seed."

Come, Thou soul-transforming Spirit,
Bless the sower and the seed;
Let each heart Thy grace inherit;
Raise the weak, the hungry feed!
From the gospel
Now supply Thy people's need.

2 Oh, may all enjoy the blessing
Which Thy word's designed to give;
Let us all, Thy love possessing,
Joyfully the truth receive;
And for ever
To Thy praise and glory live.

JONATHAN EVANS.

86   " Father, hear us!"

God Almighty and All-seeing!
Holy One, in whom we all
Live, and move, and have our being,
Hear us when on Thee we call;
Father, hear us,
As before Thy throne we fall.

2 Of all good art Thou the Giver;
Weak and wandering ones are we;
Then for ever, yea, for ever,
In Thy presence would we be;
Oh, be near us,
That we wander not from Thee.

F. S. PIERPONT.

DENNIS. S. M.   Arr. fr. H. G. NAGELI.

STILL, still with Thee, my God, I would de - sire to be:

By day, by night, at home, a - broad, I would be still with Thee.

87   "Still with Thee."

STILL, still with Thee, my God,
    I would desire to be:
By day, by night, at home, abroad,
    I would be still with Thee.

2 With Thee, when dawn comes in,
    And calls me back to care,
Each day returning to begin
    With Thee, my God, in prayer.

3 With Thee, when day is done,
    And evening calms the mind;
The setting, as the rising, sun
    With Thee my heart would find.

4 With Thee, in Thee, by faith
    Abiding I would be;
By day, by night, in life, in death,
    I would be still with Thee.
               JAMES D. BURNS

88   "He careth."

HOW GENTLE God's commands!
    How kind His precepts are!
Come, cast your burdens on the Lord,
    And trust His constant care.

2 Beneath His watchful eye
    His saints securely dwell;
That hand which bears creation up
    Shall guard His children well.

3 Why should this anxious load
    Press down your weary mind?
Haste to your heavenly Father's throne,
    And sweet refreshment find.

4 His goodness stands approved,
    Unchanged from day to day:
I 'll drop my burden at His feet,
    And bear a song away.
               PHILIP DODDRIDGE.

STOCKWELL. 8s, 7s.   D. E. Jones.

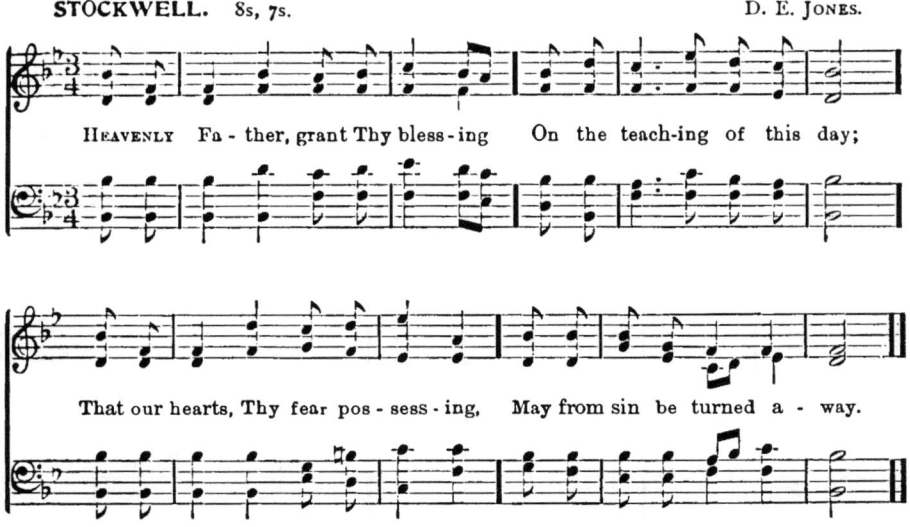

Heavenly Fa - ther, grant Thy bless - ing On the teach-ing of this day;

That our hearts, Thy fear pos - sess - ing, May from sin be turned a - way.

89   "Turn us, O Lord."

Heavenly Father, grant Thy blessing
  On the teaching of this day;
That our hearts, Thy fear possessing,
  May from sin be turned away.

2 Have we wandered? oh, forgive us,
  Have we wished from truth to rove?
Turn, oh, turn us, and receive us,
  And incline us Thee to love.

3 Through the day, Lord, Thou hast given
  Strength sufficient for our need;
Cheered us with sweet hopes of heaven,
  Helped and comforted indeed.

4 Lord, we thank Thee, and adore Thee,
  For the solace of Thy love;
And rejoicing thus before Thee,
  Wait Thy blessing from above!
                    Henry Bateman.

90   Benevolent Efforts.

Cast thy bread upon the waters,
  Thinking not 't is thrown away;
God Himself saith, thou shalt gather
  It again some future day.

2 Cast thy bread upon the waters;
  Wildly though the billows roll,
They but aid thee as thou toilest
  Truth to spread from pole to pole.

3 As the seed, by billows floated,
  To some distant island lone,
So to human souls benighted,
  That thou flingest may be borne.

4 Cast thy bread upon the waters;
  Why wilt thou still doubting stand?
Bounteous shall God send the harvest,
  If thou sow'st with liberal hand.
                Mrs P. A. Hanaford.

MANOAH.   C. M.   Arr. fr. ROSSINI.

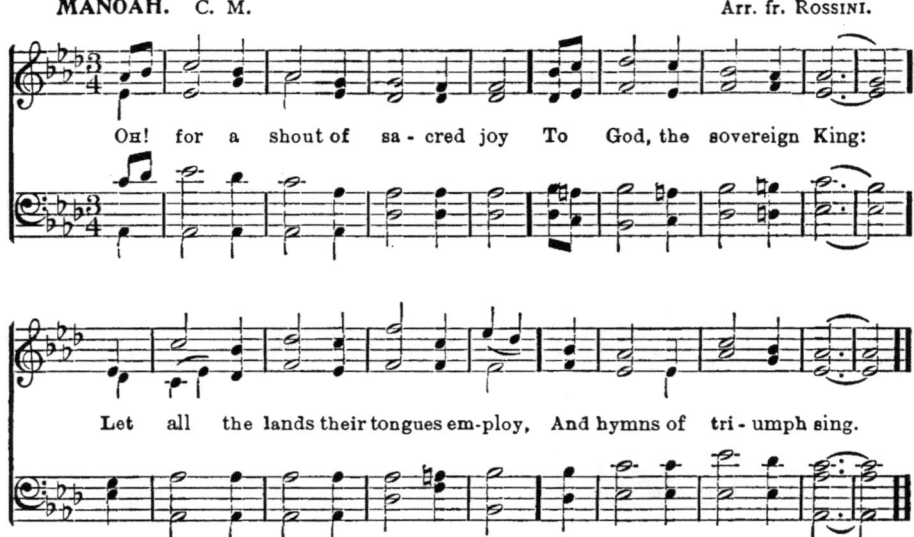

Oh! for a shout of sa-cred joy To God, the sovereign King:

Let all the lands their tongues em-ploy, And hymns of tri-umph sing.

91   "A Thoughtless Tongue."

OH! for a shout of sacred joy
　To God, the sovereign King:
Let all the lands their tongues employ,
　And hymns of triumph sing.

2 Jesus, our God, ascends on high;
　His heavenly guards around
Attend Him rising through the sky,
　With trumpets' joyful sound.

3 While angels shout and praise their King,
　Let mortals learn their strains;
Let all the earth His honor sing;—
　O'er all the earth He reigns.

4 Rehearse His praise, with awe profound;
　Let knowledge lead the song;
Nor mock Him with a solemn sound
　Upon a thoughtless tongue.

ISAAC WATTS.

92   Longing for Holiness.

OH, wherefore, Lord, doth Thy dear praise
　But tremble on my tongue?
Why lack my lips sweet skill to raise
　A full, triumphant song?

2 Oh, make me, Lord, Thy statutes learn;
　Keep in Thy ways my feet;
Then shall my lips divinely burn;
　Then shall my songs be sweet.

3 Each sin I cast away shall make
　My soul more strong to soar;
Each work I do for Thee shall wake
　A strain divine the more.

4 My voice shall more delight Thine ear,
　The more I wait on Thee;
Thy service bring my song more near
　The angelic harmony.

THOMAS H. GILL.

RAKEM. L. M. 6l. I. B. WOODBURY.

THE Lord my pas-ture shall pre-pare, And feed me with a shepherd's care;
D. C.—My noon-day walks He shall at-tend, And all my midnight hours de-.fend.

His presence shall my wants sup-ply, And guard me with a watchful eye:

93 The Good Shepherd.

THE Lord my pasture shall prepare,
And feed me with a shepherd's care;
His presence shall my wants supply,
And guard me with a watchful eye:
My noon-day walks He shall attend,
And all my midnight hours defend.

2 When in the sultry glebe I faint,
Or on the thirsty mountain pant,
To fertile vales and dewy meads,
My weary, wandering steps He leads,
Where peaceful rivers, soft and slow,
Amid the verdant landscape flow.

3 Though in a bare and rugged way,
Through devious, lonely wilds I stray,
Thy bounty shall my pains beguile,
The barren wilderness shall smile,
With sudden greens and herbage crowned,
And streams shall murmur all around.

JOSEPH ADDISON.

94 Divine and Human.

O LOVE, who formedst me to wear
The image of Thy Godhead here;
Who soughtest me with tender care
Thro' all my wanderings wild and drear;
O Love, I give myself to Thee,
Thine ever, only Thine to be.

2 O Love, who ere life's earliest dawn
On me Thy choice has gently laid;
O Love, who here as Man wast born,
And like to us in all things made:
O Love, I give myself to Thee,
Thine ever, only Thine to be.

3 O Love, who once in time wast slain,
Pierced thro' and thro' with bitter woe;
O Love, who wrestling thus didst gain
That we eternal joy might know;
O Love, I give myself to Thee,
Thine ever, only Thine to be.

C. WINKWORTH, tr.

KNOX.   C. M.

Fr. TEMPLE MELODIES.

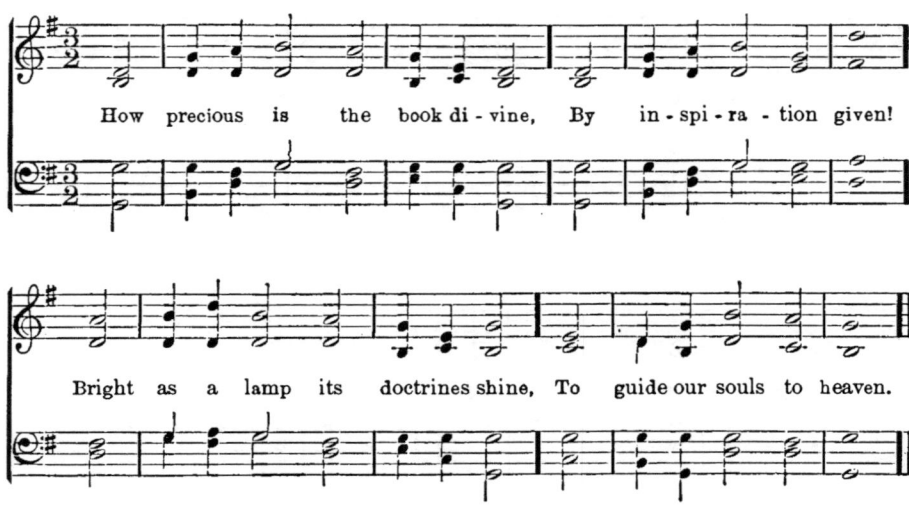

How precious is   the   book di - vine,   By   in - spi - ra - tion given!

Bright as   a   lamp its   doctrines shine, To   guide our souls to   heaven.

95   Psalm 119.

How precious is the book divine,
  By inspiration given!
Bright as a lamp its doctrines shine,
  To guide our souls to heaven.

2 O'er all the strait and narrow way
  Its radiant beams are cast;
A light whose never weary ray
  Grows brightest at the last.

3 It sweetly cheers our drooping hearts,
  In this dark vale of tears;
Life, light, and joy, it still imparts,
  And quells our rising fears.

4 This lamp, through all the tedious night
  Of life, shall guide our way,
Till we behold a clearer light
  Of an eternal day.

JOHN FAWCETT.

96   Psalm 119.

How shall the young secure their hearts,
  And guard their lives from sin?
Thy word the choicest rules imparts
  To keep the conscience clean.

2 When once it enters to the mind,
  It spreads such light abroad;
The meanest souls instruction find,
  And raise their thoughts to God.

3 'T is like the sun, a heavenly light,
  That guides us all the day;
And, through the dangers of the night,
  A lamp to lead our way.

4 Thy precepts make me truly wise;
  I hate the sinner's road;
I hate my own vain thoughts that rise,
  But love Thy law, my God!

ISAAC WATTS.

AMERICA. 6s, 4s.
H. CAREY.

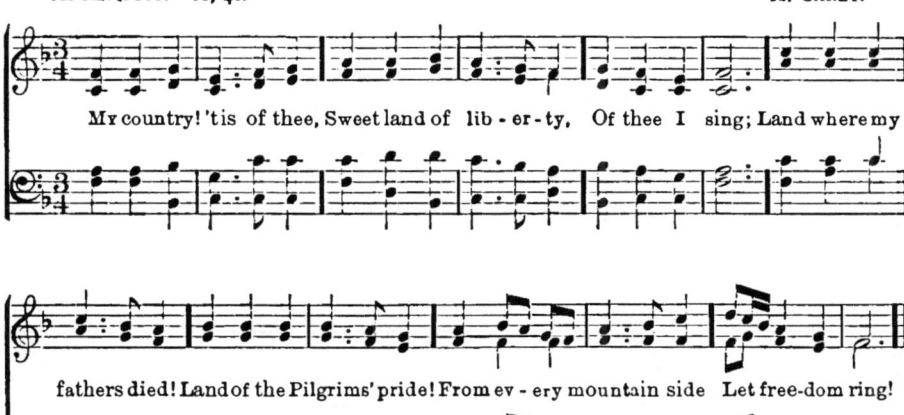

My country! 'tis of thee, Sweet land of lib - er - ty, Of thee I sing; Land where my

fathers died! Land of the Pilgrims' pride! From ev - ery mountain side Let free-dom ring!

97   National Song.

My country! 'tis of thee,
Sweet land of liberty,
   Of thee I sing;
Land where my fathers died!
Land of the Pilgrims' pride!
From every mountain side
   Let freedom ring!

2 My native country, thee—
Land of the noble, free—
   Thy name I love;
I love thy rocks and rills,
Thy woods and templed hills;
My heart with rapture thrills
   Like that above.

3 Let music swell the breeze,
And ring from all the trees
   Sweet freedom's song:
Let mortal tongues awake;
Let all that breathe partake;
Let rocks their silence break,
   The sound prolong.

4 Our fathers' God! to Thee,
Author of liberty,
   To Thee we sing:
Long may our land be bright
With freedom's holy light;
Protect us by Thy might,
   Great God, our King!

SAMUEL F. SMITH.

98   Song for our State.

GOD bless our noble State,
And make her doubly great,
   In progress grand,
Nor fear to right the wrong,
Protect among the throng
The weak as well as strong
   By her command.

2 Long may her banner bright,
Wave in the morning light,
   And all her laws,
Approved by justice stand,
Her sons a manly band,
Her daughters hand in hand,
   The home her cause.

99   LONG LIVE, LONG LIVE AMERICA.

J. E. RANKIN, D. D.   W. H. PONTIUS.

1. A - mer - i - ca, so proud and free, My song, my heart, I
2. Thou art so sweet in thy re - pose, The world thy friend, a -

give to thee! Full high thy brave, strong wing has won, Thine
bashed thy foes; Thou seek - est not the bat - tle - plain, Thy

ea - gle eye is on the sun; Still up - ward be thy heav'nward flight,
fields wave with the gold - en grain; The sheaves which thou dost gar - ner in,

Still up-ward mount, till lost in light, Still up-ward mount till lost in light.
Come with the harvest's mer - ry din, Come with the harvest's mer - ry din.

LONG LIVE, LONG LIVE AMERICA. Concluded.

A - mer - i - ca, so proud and free, My song, my heart I give to thee;

Long live, long live A - mer - i - ca! Long live, long live A - mer - i - ca.

emphatic.

3 For gladness floats on every breeze,
From city streets, from forest trees;
And when rings out toil's bell at noon,
Thy heart with joy is all in tune;
It thrills thine every vital chord,
For labor here has sure reward.

4 America, so proud and free,
I give my song, my heart to thee!
Still let thy heav'n-born symbol fly
In every clime, 'neath every sky;
Still rise a yeoman race, to stand
For God, and home and native land!

100   **THE BREAKING WAVES DASHED HIGH.**

FELICIA HEMANS.   MISS BROWNE, arr.

1. The break-ing waves dash'd high   On a stern and rock-bound coast,
2. Not as the conqueror comes,   They, the true-heart-ed came;

ALTO.

3. A - mid the storm they sang,   The stars heard and the sea!
4. What sought they thus a - far?   Bright jew-els of the mine?

From Book IV of Cecilian Series of Study and Song.

THE BREAKING WAVES DASHED HIGH. Concluded.

The woods a-gainst a storm-y sky Their gi - ant branches tossed;
Not with the roll of stir - ring drums, Or trump that sings of fame,

The sound-ing aisles of wood-land rang With an - thems of the free,
The wealth of seas, the spoils of war? They sought a faith's pure shrine!

The beav-y night hung dark, The hills and wa - ters o'er,
Nor as the fly - ing come, In si - lence and in fear,

The o - cean ea - gle soared O'er roll - ing wave's white foam,
Ay, call it ho - ly ground, The soil where first they trod;

When a band of ex - iles moor'd their bark On wild New Eng-land's shore.
They shook the depths of des - ert's gloom With hymns of loft - y cheer.

The rock - ing pines in for - est roar'd, To bid them wel - come home.
They left unstained what there they found, Free - dom to wor - ship God.

101   **FLAG OF THE FREE.**

1. Flag of the free, fair-est to see! Borne thro' the strife and the thunder of war;
2. Flag of the brave, long may it wave, Chos - en of God while His might we a - dore,

Ban-ner so bright, with star-ry light, Float ev - er proudly from mountain to shore:
In freedom's van, for good to man, Sym-bol of right thro' the years passing o'er:

Em - blem of free-dom, hope to the slave, Spread thy fair folds to shield and to save,
Pride of our coun-try, honored a - far, Scat - ter each cloud that dims but a star,

While thro' the sky loud rings the cry, Un - ion and Lib - er - ty! One ev - er - more.

102   ### COLUMBIA, THE GEM OF THE OCEAN.

1. Co - lum-bia, the gem of the o - cean! The home of the brave and the
2. When war wing'd its wide des-o - la - tion, And threat-en'd the land to de -
3. The Un-ion, the Un-ion for - ev - er, Our glo - ri - ous na - tion's sweet

free! The shrine of each pa - triot's de - vo - tion, A
form, The ark then of free-dom's foun - da - tion, Co -
hymn, May the wreaths it has won nev - er with - er, Nor the

world of - fers hom - age to thee: Thy man-dates make he - roes as -
lum - bia rode safe thro' the storm: With gar - lands of vic - t'ry a -
stars of its glo - ry grow dim, May the serv - ice u - ni - ted ne'er

sem - ble, When Lib - er - ty's form stands in view, Thy
round her, When proud - ly she bore her brave crew, With her
sev - er But they to their col - ors prove true! The

COLUMBIA, THE GEM OF THE OCEAN. Concluded.

103

THE STAR-SPANGLED BANNER.

SOPRANO.

1. { Oh,..... say, can you see, by the dawn's ear - ly light,
   { Whose broad stripes and bright stars, thro' the per - il - ous fight,

What so proud - ly we hailed at the twi - light's last gleam-ing? }
O'er the ram - parts we watched were so gal - lant - ly stream-ing? }

SOP. & ALTO.

And the rock - et's red glare, the bombs burst - ing in air,

Gave proof thro' the night that our flag was still there.

ThE STAR-SPANGLED BANNER. Concluded.

Oh,.. say, does that star - span - gled ban - ner yet wave,

O'er the land of the free and the home of the brave?

2 On that shore, dimly seen through the mists of the deep,
    Where the foe's haughty host in dread silence reposes,
What is that which the breeze, o'er the towering steep,
    As it fitfully blows, now conceals, now discloses?
Now it catches the gleam of the morning's first beam,
In full glory reflected, now shines on the stream;
           CHORUS.
'Tis the star-spangled banner! O long may it wave
O'er the land of the free and the home of the brave!

3 And where is that band who so vauntingly swore
    That the havoc of war and the battle's confusion
A home and a country should leave us no more?
    Their blood has washed out their foul footstep's pollution.
No refuge could save the hireling and slave
From the terror of flight or the gloom of the grave;
           CHORUS.
And the star-spangled banner in triumph doth wave
O'er the land of the free and the home of the brave!

4 O, thus be it ever when freemen shall stand
    Between their loved homes and war's desolation!
Blest with vict'ry and peace, may the Heaven-rescued land
    Praise the Power that hath made and preserved us a nation.
Then conquer we must, when our cause it is just,
And this be our motto, "In God is our trust";
           CHORUS.
And the star-spangled banner in triumph shall wave
O'er the land of the free and the home of the brave!

FRANCIS SCOTT KEY.

INDEX OF FIRST LINES.

Lightning Source UK Ltd.
Milton Keynes UK
UKHW050011080119
334942UK00006BA/228/P